HOW TO GET AHEAD IN HR

HOW TO GET AHEAD IN HR

KAY MADDOX-DAINES

LONDON PUBLISHING PARTNERSHIP

Published by London Publishing Partnership
www.londonpublishingpartnership.co.uk

ISBN: 978-1-913019-45-7 (pbk)
ISBN: 978-1-913019-46-4 (iPDF)
ISBN: 978-1-913019-47-1 (ePUB)

A catalogue record for this book is
available from the British Library

This book has been composed in
Kepler Std

Copy-edited and typeset by
T&T Productions Ltd, London
www.tandtproductions.com

Printed and bound in Great Britain
by Page Bros

Cover image

Why wires? HR reaches every corner of an organization, connecting individuals and teams by getting the right people in the right place at the right time. An organization's people professionals carry signals across it, through policy development and communication that impact company culture, change, employee engagement and productivity. People professionals are an integral part of a wired network that facilitates employee development, provides equity in compensation and rewards, and enables productivity. We also chose this particular image because it is dynamic and suggests diversity – both of which are important facets of any good HR department!

CONTENTS

ACKNOWLEDGEMENTS

FIRSTLY, TO ALASTAIR, FOR KEEPING everything going and for his unwavering support in everything I do; and to Beth, for her independence, self-motivation and drive.

The help of my students, both past and present, is gratefully acknowledged; without their enquiring minds and career navigation questions, the idea for this book would not have been conceived. I am also very grateful to the many people professionals who have shared their experiences and to the careers coaches who have kindly shared their advice.

Thanks also to Sarah Carrington of T&T Productions Ltd for her thorough and sympathetic copy-editing, and to Sam Clark and Richard Baggaley of London Publishing Partnership for their support and patience in weaving this book into its publishable form.

INTRODUCTION

WHAT IS THIS BOOK ABOUT and who is it for?

Over the course of my career I have worked in people management as a consultant, a manager and an educator, and there is one question I have been asked more than any other: 'How do I get a job in HR?' I scanned the available resources looking for a text I could point my students to, but no single book provided all the answers and supported every possible individual background. I failed to find that one text that would provide insights into how to get qualified *and* what level to get qualified at; that would give details about international people careers *and* how to get work experience in the profession; that would give clear advice about the different roles in the people profession *and* how to progress. This book aims to fill that gap.

I refer to both the people profession and HR in this book. I note in chapter 1 how the profession has evolved, and I challenge the terminology used to describe the role of the contemporary people professional. The term HR is now dated but I use it interchangeably with people profession for ease of reference and familiarity throughout the book. Although many forward-looking organizations such as Virgin Atlantic, Formula E Holdings, Zoopla, Tesco and Google have appointed chief people officers to lead on all matters relating to people in their organizations, many businesses have retained the more traditional role of Director of HR. Language evolves slowly and we are currently in an era of evolution.

One of the many great aspects of the people profession is the ability for people to join at various points in their career. There are opportunities for those at the beginning of their careers and for those in transition. In this book I provide guidance for school leavers, graduates and career changers, and for people of all ages and levels of experience. I also discuss how to progress in HR to help those seeking their next HR role.

I believe that there has never been a more exciting time to join the people profession. A career in HR has always presented variety and a good mix of opportunities, but the profession is changing quickly and this calls for a diverse range of skills, knowledge and competence. People professionals will need to support organizations in managing people differently, through virtual and hybrid working arrangements. This calls for expertise in digitalization, analytics, internationalization and value-based decision-making. People professionals will increasingly be needed to guide organizations through significant change, moving beyond discussions of workforce engagement to more of a partnership approach, whereby every employee is able to contribute fully to the goals of the organization.

A career in the people profession provides plenty of opportunities for progression and advancement, and this will develop further as the profession evolves. The knowledge, skills and competencies that are needed today may well change over time. Specialisms are likely to develop further to take account of the need for skilled analysts and digital experts. Whether you have a preference for learning and development, compensation and reward, organizational design and development, strategic planning, operational people management, resourcing talent, performance management, health and well-being, or technology and analysis, there is a role for you in the people profession! Not only that but the pay is pretty good too, as I discuss further in chapter 1.

Beyond pay, the profession offers the opportunity to make a difference to people and to organizations, to challenge taken-for-granted assumptions and to engage in meaningful work. The skills, knowledge and experience that you gain in the people profession are highly transferable too, so that if you later decide to change career you will have developed a set of versatile competencies that will support you in a wide range of roles.

This book provides details about how the HR profession is evolving, and, using a range of skills-based exercises, quizzes and reflective activities, it will help you prepare for your ideal role. Each chapter provides a variety of case study examples and a summary of actions to help you get started. I discuss some of the most well-known HR professional bodies, how to get qualified and which level of the profession is right for you. The job search chapter contains a variety of CV examples and some top tips from recruiters who specialize in HR.

For those already working in HR, the book provides advice on how to get promoted and advance in your career. It offers insights into how the profession is evolving and looks at the opportunities that are available. Being aware of the changes that lie ahead of you will help you future-proof your career. A whole chapter of the book is dedicated to continuing professional development to help you focus on your career goals.

The book can be read in any order and there may be chapters that you wish to prioritize depending on your preferences and goals. A summary of each chapter is listed below.

Chapter 1. The evolution of HR

From personnel to HR and now to people management, chapter 1 provides an overview of the evolution of HR and what this has meant for those working in the profession. The structure of work is briefly explored alongside the development of the profession, from the Industrial Revolution, through the industrial relations phase, to personnel, HR and strategic business partnering.

Chapter 2. Is HR right for you?

Here I explore the various roles in HR: the usual job titles and what HR people do. From generalist HR roles at assistant, advisor, partner, manager and director level to specialist roles in talent development, HR analytics, organizational development and compensation and reward, case study examples support readers to understand the various professional roles available.

Chapter 3. HR professional bodies

In this chapter we will explore and compare the two biggest HR professional bodies: the Society for Human Resource Management (SHRM) in the US and the Chartered Institute of Personnel and Development (CIPD) in the UK. We will also look at three smaller professional bodies: namely, the Singapore Human Resources Institute (SHRI), the Institute of Human Resource Management Practitioners (IHRMP) in Ghana, and the Australian HR Institute (AHRI). We will assess what they have to offer and look at their membership requirements, as well as investigating their progression routes and accreditation.

Chapter 4. Getting qualified

This chapter introduces certification requirements across five different people management professional bodies: the SHRM, the CIPD, the SHRI, the IHRMP and the AHRI. It discusses the eligibility criteria for certification via qualifications and experience and it also discusses the entry points for certification based on qualifications and people management experience.

Chapter 5. HR for school leavers and graduates

HR as a career offers a number of possible entry points. Chapter 5 discusses the opportunities for both school leavers and graduates. In England, for example, HR level 3 apprenticeships are open to school leavers aged 16 and over while HR level 5 apprenticeships are open for those aged 18 or over. In the US it is more likely that you will have a degree or a few years' work experience prior to transitioning to human resource management (HRM). Various degree subjects are explored in relation to preparation for a career in HR along with professional body accreditations that may or may not be included in the degree.

Chapter 6. HR for career changers

It is never too late to transition to a new role, and having some previous work experience can work to your advantage in the people profession. A great way to prepare for a career change is to explore job profiles and their entry requirements. This will provide you with a platform from which to assess where you are and where you wish to get to. This chapter provides insights into transferable skills and uses case study examples to reveal how others have made the transition. Various roles are considered across the public, private and third sectors to help you identify not only opportunities that await you but also at what level to pitch your applications for entry into the profession.

Chapter 7. The job search

For some this will be the first role they ever apply for; for others it may have been some time since they applied for a job. Chapter 7 provides some useful practice tips from specialist HR recruiters on how to prepare a CV and how to target specific vacancies. It also explores other ways in which a new role might be secured, most likely through the power of networks. An introduction to how networking can support job hunting is provided, focusing on LinkedIn as a tool for connecting with old and new contacts and developing your relationships with them. CV templates are provided for both generalist and specialist HR roles.

Chapter 8. Interviews and selection tests

Preparing for a job interview is a vital part of the job search process, and it entails much more than deciding what to say and how to present yourself. This chapter provides top tips for making a good impression, starting with research to find out more about the organization and role in question. Getting to know the organization, its vision, mission, strategic objectives and values can help candidates prepare potential questions that can be asked at the end of the interview. Interview techniques, competency-based questions, psychometric testing and different employer approaches are discussed. The process of first, second and subsequent interviews alongside presentations and other selection tests is explained with examples and case studies.

Chapter 9. The future of HR

The HR landscape is evolving quickly through technological developments that are changing the way HR professionals work and manage. Although HR analytics has been available for some time, very few HR professionals are getting the most out of the data available to them. This presents new opportunities for those seeking to enter the profession and for those looking to progress. Data analytics supports HR in analysing data and discovering new insights. Robotic process automation (RPA), artificial intelligence (AI) and virtual reality (VR) are already having an impact on the available tools, systems and infrastructures across a range of business functions, including HR. Automation of transactional processes such as applicant tracking, employee databases and documentation allows HR to focus on gaining better insights into employee experience and engagement, as well as new work landscapes and new workflows. This requires new skills and knowledge, and ultimately it means the creation of new roles in HR. It is these opportunities that form the focus of this chapter.

Chapter 10. Continuing professional development and career progression

Chapter 10 explores continuing professional development (CPD) and how this supports career progression. It discusses the various ways in which CPD can be undertaken and also how to look back and reflect on past activities to inform the compilation of a plan that supports career advancement. A variety of CPD templates is included and we discuss each one. The last section of the book focuses on 'looking ahead to stay ahead', which helps people professionals ensure that their skills and knowledge are continually updated and helps them plan not just their next career move but ultimately how to achieve their dream role.

Chapter 11. Further resources and support

This final chapter provides details of follow-up support and guidance that you may find helpful to understand more about the people profession and how to move forward in your career. It includes recommendations relating to books, social media, websites, Ted Talks, podcasts, You Tube and other media, with links given for useful sources.

I do hope you find this book a helpful guide to getting started or promoted in the people profession. The fast-changing nature of businesses and organizations will provide many new opportunities, and the available roles will undoubtedly evolve. My own view is that it is a very exciting time to be working in the people profession. I wish you well with your career.

Chapter 1

THE EVOLUTION OF HR

THE NOTION OF PEOPLE MANAGEMENT has been around for thousands of years. In prehistoric times tribal leaders were selected according to specified criteria such as wisdom and skill. The Romans were led by centurions who provided accountability through a hierarchical system. The development of leadership and management traces its roots to the military, where effective armies required leaders that could engage their troops through a shared vision of success and effective recruitment, selection and development. In early ancient times emperors reigned over communes and villages, collecting taxes and providing safety to citizens, which required effective leadership and the allocation of specific roles and responsibilities. As long ago as 2000 BCE the Chinese used employee screening techniques, and the ancient Greeks were also known for their apprenticeship systems. But these early examples of what we now term people management tended to be duties performed by supervisors and line managers rather than as part of a specialist role.

In this chapter we review the development of the people profession from the early 1900s to the present day. We explore how key developments have informed the roles that we see advertised. The profession as we now know it has evolved in relation to external events, including political, economic and social factors. For example, the world population has increased from 1.8 billion people in 1919 to 7.6 billion people in 2021. High-speed technology in the field of communication has completely changed the nature of education, commerce, banking, agriculture and health, and technological developments have accelerated globalization and the nature of business and competition.

THE BEGINNING OF PERSONNEL MANAGEMENT

In recognition of the harshness of industrial conditions and under the influence of both trade unions and Quakers, who campaigned for improvements in industrial practice, the role of welfare officer was created at the end of the nineteenth century. These roles were occupied by women and they predominantly focused on the protection of women and girls. As the roles became more established there was some tension between balancing the remit of moral protection officer with the need for higher output in production. The Chartered Institute of Personnel and Development can trace its roots back to the Welfare Workers' Association, established in 1913 with thirty-four members.[1]

World War I saw a major development in the direction of personnel management when women were recruited in large numbers to fill vacant roles as men left to fight. This meant reaching agreement with trade unions about the recruitment of unskilled women into craftsmen's jobs. In the 1920s and 1930s specific new roles were created to manage employment matters, with a focus on handling absence, recruitment, dismissal and pay issues. Employer federations negotiated national pay rates with trade unions, although there were local variations.

World War II saw the development of new full-time roles in welfare and personnel work in all establishments that produced war materials. The government identified this role as vital to improving efficiency, and in 1943 there were around 5,300 people working with a personnel function. The main focus during the war years was on implementing rules in support of state-governed production, and as a result the emerging profession of personnel had its foundation in bureaucracy.

What is personnel?

Over time personnel grew to be much more than just a welfare role. Frameworks of policies and procedures were developed to manage the employment relationship between employer and employee. Successive UK governments actively encouraged the appointment of personnel officers (particularly in industries nationalized in the 1940s) to ensure smooth management of the employment relationship in unionized environments.

Formalized, standardized and integrated sets of policies and practices for effectively managing people in the workplace began to appear. This dedicated function brought coordinated approaches to recruitment, selection, induction, training, promotion and discipline as well as reporting and appeals mechanisms. The growth of discipline provided more efficient employer coordination and control of employees as organizations grew in size and complexity. Characterized by routine and administration, personnel roles are about supporting increasing production in pursuit of organizational goals.

There were three models of personnel.[2] First, there was the clerk of works, a low-level role with general responsibility for personnel, focusing on administration and welfare. Second, there was the contracts manager, who was responsible for the implementation of well-established procedures and agreements with a close alignment to industrial relations. Third, there was the architect, who played a key role by establishing strategic policies to support corporate objectives and by designing personnel activities through a framework of delegating tasks to line managers in order to free up time for strategic activities.

The posibility of developing a strategic focus through an architect-type role in personnel was considered to be a significant challenge. The potential to support strategic activities depends on the extent to which personnel is involved in planning, which can be limited by both time and volume of work, as well as the readiness of senior management to recognize the function as a key contributor to business strategy. Time away from core personnel work can impact on efficiency and effectiveness, and this creates a negative impression of capability when things do not get done, reinforcing the prejudices of senior management about personnel being a non-core function.

The key criticism of personnel is that there was only a weak relationship between the various recruiting and development activities and the overall organizational objectives. The reactive and sometimes ad hoc approach taken by personnel in relation to industrial relations issues reinforced this lack of alignment. The reluctance of senior managers to involve personnel in strategic decision making made planning difficult and added to the challenges of managing industrial relations effectively. Without access to key business information, the personnel department remained marginalized, with little opportunity to prove its worth to the organization.

Trade unions

Trade union representation was the key voice for workers up to the 1980s.[3] At the peak of union power in 1979, a total of 13.3 million trade union members – equating to 54% of the working population – were represented by 300,000 workplace representatives or 'shop stewards'. The expanding membership provided the unions with significant political influence and power. There was an upsurge in industrial action, meaning that public policy became preoccupied with managing the shop floor. The key concern was how to manage the power and influence of the unions while tackling the economic issues of the time, particularly unions' restrictive practices (e.g. closed shops that restricted new jobs to union members, practices that restricted output, or practices that hindered management from implementing efficiencies). Trade union membership now accounts for just over a quarter (26%) of the workforce.

Since the Industrial Revolution workers have been withholding labour as a means of securing improved pay and conditions. More than 40 million working days were lost in a year in 1912 as a result of the national coal strike, which saw a million miners seeking a guarantee of a minimum wage. The government intervened and ended the strike by passing the Coal Mines (Minimum Wage) Act 1912, but strikes followed from shipbuilding and engineering workers, transport workers and heavy-industry workers, all of whom were seeking improvements in pay, conditions and working hours. The 1926 general strike saw 162 million working days being lost through the actions of 1.5 million workers striking in support of the coal miners (the Trades Dispute Act banned sympathy strikes in 1927). The UK miners' strike in 1972 saw nearly 24 million working days lost and a three-day week introduced to save electricity. Widespread public sector strikes were enacted in 1979 in response to the government capping pay in an attempt to tackle inflation. This resulted in the Winter of Discontent, which saw another 29 million working days lost. Margaret Thatcher's Conservative government won a landslide victory in the same year as they promised to deliver legislation to restrict trade union power.[4] The Thatcher years restored managers' confidence by tackling militant trade unions in the automobile, mining and print industries. All were weakened during Thatcher's tenure.

In the 1960s and 1970s the personnel function evolved, using theories from the social sciences about motivation and organizational behaviour to inform its direction. Selection testing became more widely used, and formalized management development was expanded to support the skills and knowledge development of leaders and aspiring leaders. During the 1970s, specialisms such as 'reward' and 'resourcing' started to appear as discrete roles.

A new challenge for personnel

In order for personnel to effectively negotiate and manage employer–employee relations, changes were required. Personnel required additional training if it was to be able to fulfil its potential. The function needed to upskill so that it was capable of formulating workplace policies and procedural frameworks to ensure alignment with corporate policy, e.g. employee planning, selection techniques, employee development techniques and performance management systems. It also needed to be able to provide advice, guidance and training on all people matters (employment law, equal opportunities, appraisals) to line managers. Without expertise, the people function was not going to be taken seriously by senior management teams.

In 1946 the Institute of Personnel Management (IPM) was formed from the previous welfare and labour management movement. In 1955 the IPM introduced restrictions on its membership, requiring members to pass an examination, with a formal programme of education introduced and run externally by colleges. The institute recognized the need for upskilling both its members and the profession as a whole. In 1994 the IPM merged with the Institute of Training and Development, gaining chartered status in 2000 and subsequently becoming what is now the Chartered Institute of Personnel and Development (CIPD). It was not until 2009 that a common set of profession competencies was launched in the form of the HR profession map.

At this point let us consider the evolution of management and leadership theory as it is closely aligned with the way in which the people management profession has developed. Here is a very brief overview.

Traditional management

Frederick Winslow Taylor is widely recognized as one of the first management consultants. With a background in mechanical engineering and general management he published *The Principles of Scientific Management* in 1911.[5] Known as the father of scientific management, he examined how work processes could be optimized to improve the productivity of workers, and thereby their contribution to the effectiveness of their organization. He focused on recruitment and selection, job design and efficiency measures, and he highlighted that incumbents should be suited to the jobs they are doing. Taylor's work emphasized the division of labour between managers and workers, which provided the seed for Max Weber's bureaucratic organization structure.

Bureaucracy

Max Weber was a German sociologist and political economist. He argued that bureaucracy was the most efficient and rational model for the operation of a business. In 1922 he published *Economy and Society*, in which he described ideal types of public administration and governance. Weber's bureaucracy is characterized by task specialization, whereby efficiency is maximized by assigning tasks based on team members' competencies. Furthermore, he advocated management layers in the hierarchy; formal employee selection rules in accordance with skills, technical competencies and efficiency; and uniform requirements so that everyone knew what was expected of them. He stressed that relationships between employees should be solely professional, to promote decision making and rational thinking, and that promotions should be based only on achievement, experience and technical qualifications.

Human relations approach

While classical theorists focused on structures, physical working conditions, work methods, measurements and rules, the human relations movement found that social aspects of the workplace were important too. The Hawthorne studies were undertaken between 1924 and 1936 at the Hawthorne plant of the Western Electric Company in Chicago. The purpose of the studies was to find out how different aspects of the work environment – things such as lighting, the timing of breaks and the length of the working day – impacted on worker productivity. The research found that workers were more responsive to social factors, such as the people they worked with in a team and the interest the manager took in their work, than to the external environment. It was not until the Hawthorne experiments that employees were consulted about their physical working conditions and their attitude to supervisors.

Social–technical system

The Tavistock Institute of Human Relations in London carried out research to understand work groups and tasks involving 'longwall' mining techniques, which were introduced into County Durham coal fields in the 1940s. These new processes transformed 'narrow-face' mining techniques into longwall faces while also introducing new – larger and more efficient – equipment. This enabled long rectangular blocks of coal to be extracted in a single continuous operation through an automated process. This upset the social balance of the work groups, impacting morale and increasing absenteeism. Tightly knit social groups had been split up and this had a negative impact on communication. The implementation of the differential bonus system exacerbated the impact of change. This research highlighted that an organization is both a social system and a technical one, and this needs to be taken into account when managing people.

Hierarchy of needs

Abraham Maslow first introduced his concept of the hierarchy of needs in his 1943 paper 'A theory of motivation' and in his book *Motivation and Personality*.[6] Maslow believed that each and every one of us has an inbuilt desire to reach our full potential. In order to do so, however, he argued that a number of basic needs must be in place. The first basic needs are air, food, water, shelter and clothing. These are followed by security and safety, including health and wellness, financial security and safety against accidents and injury. Next, Maslow argued, we have social needs: love, acceptance and belonging, in terms of friendships, romantic attachments, family, social and community groups and religious organizations. Only when these elements are in place can we focus on our 'esteem needs', which include respect and appreciation of others, participation in professional activities, academic accomplishments, athletic or team participation and personal hobbies. At the top of Maslow's pyramid we have 'self-actualization needs', which describe our desire to fully exploit our talents, capabilities and potential.

Maslow argued that esteem needs become important when the bottom three basic needs are met. From a management perspective, this model is useful for shaping the conditions that allow people to reach their potential. Managers can identify the needs of their staff and help them feel fulfilled through work or flexible working so they can pursue interests outside of the workplace. Although Maslow's hierarchy of needs has been criticized for its unscientific approach and the lack of evidence to support a true hierarchy of needs, it has been instrumental in managing people in the workplace because it recognizes the varying factors that have an impact on motivation.

What is human resource management?

Driven by economic pressures, increased market competition and the advancement of technology, industry changed rapidly during the second half of the twentieth century. There was a very strong desire to reform conventional industrial relations in the UK; Margaret Thatcher's push for privatization and anti-union legislation accompanied a restructuring of the economy. There was a rapid decline in old industries and a rise in the service sector, with new industries that were built on high-tech products and services being free of historical industrial-relations baggage. The US excellence literature espoused examples of successful leading-edge companies, noting employee motivation, commitment and empowerment as key elements in what was to become human resource management (HRM). As competition from Asia intensified, and with slow economic growth in the Western developed nations, the focus now was on how personnel could support performance. Managers were still managing based on traditional theories of leadership and management, so HRM principles provided a platform for managing global competition.

HRM principles were introduced into British organizations in the 1980s. Initially, there was some confusion about the difference between personnel and HRM. Indeed, I remember a whole assignment dedicated to this debate when I was doing my postgraduate diploma in HRM in the mid 1990s. While personnel emphasized clear rules, HRM focused on a 'can do' attitude. Personnel was synonymous with bureaucracy and slow decision making; HRM was known for fast decisions and getting things done. Personnel management was embedded in models of negotiation, whereas HRM emphasized facilitation. When it came to rewards, personnel was aligned with fixed pay grades but HRM focused on rewarding performance. In practice, these differences and similarities could not be identified in a single organization and there are still lingering examples of personnel in many organizations today. The most important thing to note is that by integrating HRM into business strategy it was possible to align employment practices and achieve competitive advantage. In this respect, the sector moved from being reactive, prescriptive and administratively driven with personnel, to being based on proactive, descriptive and executive principles with HRM. Whereas personnel generally referred to the way in which the function managed the work-related needs of the workforce, HRM focused on the strategic contribution that employees could make to an organization. The ability to ensure that people had the right skills for the role at the right time, along with knowledge of associated costs, was of key importance to HR decisions.

As HRM became more embedded in organizations, the nature of job titles within departments began to change, from personnel officer/manager to HR advisor/manager. However, beyond the titles the actual roles took much longer to evolve into pathways that genuinely embraced the nature of the HR role and the alignment of strategic corporate goals.

Employee performance is inextricably linked to the success of an organization, and the way in which HRM supports the delivery of objectives can be viewed from two different perspectives: hard HRM and soft HRM. In hard HRM, human resources are acquired, deployed and dispensed as corporate initiatives demand. There is an emphasis on quantitative data to manage employee numbers and costs, with little regard for the needs of the human resources themselves. In comparison, soft HRM acknowledges that to gain competitive advantage the workforce must be nurtured and developed, whether they are full time or part time, temporary workers or on a contract. In reality, organizations are likely to lean towards both hard and soft approaches at different times. When the focus is on cost minimization, emphasizing lean production, labour is more likely to be considered a resource. Ensuring effective alignment of HRM policies and organizational goals encourages a focus on values, trust, commitment and communication to ensure effective work processes.

The term 'human resources' as a way to describe employees has been contentious ever since HRM arrived from the US. Some consider the term to be negative, questioning whether it is appropriate to treat people in the same way as any other resource that is required to deliver performance outcomes. The term 'resources' tends to be used to describe services, equipment, materials, money, space, time and so on. Some people argue that the term is dehumanizing since it fails to recognize the personal qualities of each member of staff. Others focus on how an organization's performance is dependent on harnessing the value of employees through investment and by securing commitment to organizational goals – focusing, therefore, on the philosophy rather than the terminology.

In any case, HRM is evolving quickly, with the most forward-thinking companies now focusing on 'people practices' rather than human resources. Whereas HR was traditionally told about decisions and expected to execute them, people professionals are consulted and are involved in strategic conversations to support organizational strategic goals.

THE EVOLUTION OF THE PEOPLE PROFESSION

The people profession has evolved considerably over the last century and has done so even more rapidly over the last 30 years. The pace of change has accelerated; new professional roles are emerging, and both new ways of working and new priorities are evolving. The focus is now moving away from the classification of humans as a resource, the administrative burden of personnel and the over-reliance on generic best practices and processes and is instead moving towards outcome-driven perspectives. New emphasis is driving the people agenda, from concepts such as corporate purpose and organizational culture and behaviours, creating responsible organizations made up of diverse and inclusive workforces that support well-being, culture change and the development and alignment of people with business strategy. Let us review some of the key areas that are shaping the current people agenda.

Globalization

Participation in the world's global markets is not new; indeed, internationalization and the transfer of goods across geographic borders has been part of business life since the Industrial Revolution. Technology has increased the ability to trade at a phenomenal rate, transforming the way many organizations do business. Globalization has widened the marketplace for both sellers and buyers, with new electronic payment systems supporting the world as a customer base. Globalization has also brought a significant increase in competition, with companies that once competed locally and nationally now finding themselves operating in a global marketplace. From a people management perspective, professionals must now adapt their thinking and practices to include cultural differences, foreign regulations and technological developments. The influence and implication of operating globally depends on the type of organization, its product lifecycle and its approach to people practice.

Technology

Rapid technological developments have meant that some of the routine transactional elements of people management – tracking sickness absence, updating employee information, compiling turnover reports, tracking applicants and analysing key data, for example – can now be carried out through sophisticated information systems. This allows people management to focus on more complex people matters and on adding value. Virtual and augmented reality is continuing to mature, providing opportunities for onboarding and training to be transformed so that participants can really experience learning, e.g. through virtual transportation to different countries in support of cultural training. Machine learning applications in people management focus on predictive analysis and talent relationships, and they are used mostly in the recruitment process.

People analytics

People analytics refers to the data-driven and goal-focused approach to exploring people processes, functions, challenges and opportunities in order to solve business problems. People analytics uses people's data, collected through HR systems (payroll, absence, etc.), and business information (performance data) to gather insights to improve evidenced-based decision making. By investigating data, it is possible to explore cause and correlation to determine relationships that support decision making, all enabled by computer programs and modelling techniques. Taking a strategic and planned approach to people analytics is likely to create the most value and will demonstrate the people management return on investment.

Corporate responsibility

Corporate responsibility refers to the impact that an organization has on society, the environment and the economy. It is about the ethics that drive business activities and the way in which an organization operates. People professionals are integral to the way in which organizations build and maintain ethical cultures, and this refers to all aspects of people practice, from compliance with minimum statutory obligations to good and fair practice in business decisions. From recruitment, terms and conditions, communications, diversity, learning and development to performance and reward, people professionals are integral to building ethical cultures. The people function has a role in communicating with employees across their organization and educating them about their responsibilities in both social and environmental matters.

Health, safety and well-being

Promoting well-being at work can help prevent stress and create positive working environments for staff. The health and well-being of individuals is key to employee engagement and organizational performance. However, well-being initiatives need to be directly aligned with organizational strategy in order to benefit from reduced sickness absence and higher productivity. This includes close alignment of well-being strategies with health and safety policies. Risks to employee health from physical hazards have decreased significantly since the introduction of the Health and Safety at Work Act 1974, but there has been a rise in the number of reported mental health issues over the last decade, with the main risk to employees' health at work now recognized as being psychological. People professionals integrate well-being practices into their organization's day-to-day operations, working with senior managers to ensure that this is regarded as a priority and communicating the benefits to line managers. They ensure that policies and practices are implemented consistently.

Human capital

Human capital refers to the economic value of employees' experience and skills, including not only their education, training, intelligence, skills and health but also their loyalty and punctuality. People professionals are concerned with ensuring that individuals have the capability to maximize the value that organizations, people and society generate from work. Organizations that secure competitive advantage based on their unique resources, i.e. knowledge, cite human capital as fundamental to delivering value to key stakeholders. People professionals can support organizations by ensuring that cognitive skills such as understanding and reasoning are included in corporate training and development alongside non-cognitive skills such as interpersonal skills and teamwork. Training programmes work most effectively when they include both generic and organization-specific development and when employees are engaged in selecting appropriate programmes for themselves.

Agile working

Agile working empowers people to work where, when and how they choose, maximizing flexibility and focusing on performance and outcomes. It is about bringing people, technology, time and connectivity together in order to deliver results. People professionals can support agile working through the development of organizational structures that support cross-functional working, open technology that promotes knowledge-sharing from outside of the organization, and non-hierarchical structures that promote effective collaboration and self-directed work groups. Job design is effective when linked solely to output, not to fixed hours, and where leadership and management foster involvement and participation. People professionals are integral to the design of agile working practices. They need to consider how agile teams can be created, how to motivate behaviour change from individual performance to team collaboration, and how people can advance in their organization.

Equality, diversity and inclusivity

Equality in the workplace refers to equal opportunities and fairness for employees and job applicants: people should not be treated differently for any reason protected by discrimination law. The Equality Act covers the same groups that were protected by existing equality legislation: age, disability, gender reassignment, race, religion or belief, sex, sexual orientation, marriage and civil partnership and pregnancy and maternity. These are now called 'protected characteristics'. Diversity and inclusion go beyond the legislative requirements, ensuring that differences are embraced and individuals can flourish. People professionals are well placed to support the development of an inclusive culture within an organization and to sometimes challenge stakeholders, through difficult conversations, in order to drive change. People professionals are key to raising awareness of diversity and inclusion and in initiating training programmes to support organizations in this area. They review job advertisements for gendered or other biased wording, check that flexible working policies are effective, examine recruitment data to understand how diverse each stage of the selection process is, and ensure that organizational policies treat people fairly. People professionals are also instrumental in supporting hiring managers and ensuring that they are trained, as well as reviewing pay, progression and employee survey feedback to identify any barriers that may prevent people from flourishing within their organization.

THE PEOPLE PROFESSION SURVEY 2020: UK AND IRELAND

The CIPD carry out a survey of people professionals every year to ascertain how they are feeling and what they are focusing on. In 2020 YouGov conducted the survey online for the CIPD (in association with Workday) with a sample size of 1,368 people professionals and 204 independent professionals. The survey concluded that the people profession offers a highly rewarding career, with most respondents indicating that their careers were meaningful.

People professionals are navigating an increasingly complex and challenging world of work. The biggest drivers of change are digital transformation, organizational agility and economic pressures. The Covid-19 pandemic prioritized employee health and well-being, with many organizations allocating dedicated people professionals to monitoring employee well-being and assisting leaders with managing effectively.

The link between people strategy and business outcomes continues to be a high priority as people professionals align professional practice with organizational performance. It is sometimes difficult to balance operational efficiency and strategic delivery due to finite resources and limited time. The way in which people professionals can add value to corporate goals will continue to vary according to an organization's structure, size and sector, as well as the impact of stakeholders. Digital transformation is particularly significant for those working in larger organizations. People analytics and data skills are becoming a necessity, and practitioners need to focus on building capability in this area to meet demand.

People professionals are increasingly looking beyond how to engage employees to considering the whole employee lifecycle, prioritizing a positive working experience. Building relationships with colleagues and understanding their priorities is essential if one is to add value. This includes coaching line managers so that they are both competent and confident in delivering effective people practice. In order to effectively manage the pace of change, people professionals recognize that continuing professional development in data insights and analytics is a key priority.

SUMMARY

The effective management of people has been a concern of leaders for many years, and yet formal recognition of people management as a profession is relatively new. Over the past century, the job's evolution has been rapid: originally a welfare officer position; then a reactive personnel administration function; later a human resources approach; and, more recently, a proactive business partner and people professional. The extent to which the people professional is able to work strategically is impacted by the role and by the size, sector and lifecycle of the organization in which they work. The way in which people are managed in organizations is aligned with organizational culture and management; leadership theory can help us understand how people practice has evolved. Many organizations today invest considerable sums in ensuring an effective employee experience for all their people at every stage of the employment lifecycle. The people profession has come a long way from its welfare origins.

Chapter 2

IS HR RIGHT FOR YOU?

ASSUMING YOU HAVE MADE THE decision to pursue a career in HR, where do you begin? The answer depends, of course, on where you are starting from. Some of you will have accrued valuable work experience in other sectors and industries; for others, this may be your first role. The great thing about the HR profession is that it offers considerable flexibility, so that no matter your background there will be an opportunity for you – over the years I have worked with thousands of students from a wide range of backgrounds, from hotel receptionists seeking to gain a role as an HR Administrator to teachers, accountants and lawyers seeking a career change.

Having decided that HR is for you, you might now consider whether you would prefer to generalize or specialize. By this I mean, would you like to work across all areas in HR or would you prefer to focus on, say, resourcing talent or learning and development? To help with this decision let us first explore what HR professionals do.

The role of the HR professional spans the employee lifecycle: from recruiting, selecting, onboarding and induction to learning and developing, performance managing, well-being and employee exit. But as HR professionals become more senior in their organizations, they also become strategic partners, contributing to the development and accomplishment of organizational goals. They support the development of an organization's culture, which in turn facilitates employee engagement through employee development opportunities, recognition and reward, and well-being. HR professionals are also 'change champions', monitoring employee satisfaction, measuring the results of organization initiatives and advocating an organization's vision, mission and objectives.

In order to support the effective delivery of these tasks, the HR team is likely to include a mix of generalist and specialist HR roles. Table 1 provides some examples of likely job roles in both areas.

Table 1 Generalist and specialist roles in HR.

Generalist roles	Specialist roles
HR Administrator/Assistant	Organization Design Consultant
HR Officer/Advisor/Business Partner/ Operations Specialist	Learning and Development Manager
	Organization Development Manager
HR Manager/Head of HR/ HR People and Engagement Manager	Reward Business Partner/Analyst/ Specialist
	Employer Relations Advisor/Specialist
Interim HR Consultant (Policy)	HR Data Business Analyst/Data Manager
Director of HR/People and Organizational Development/ People and Support Services/ People and Talent Director	Talent Acquisition Manager
	HR Consultant (Advisory and Well-being)
	Employee Engagement Manager
Deputy Director of People	Human Resources Information Systems Manager/Lead/Advisor/Officer

But what do these job titles actually mean? Let us explore some case study examples of HR professionals working at a variety of levels in different organizational contexts.

Case study: Rik

Job title: HR Assistant

Rik left school with A levels in Business, English and Sociology. He tried a few roles in sales and marketing before deciding on a career in HR. Now in his early twenties, Rik has been in post for 12 months. He works for a housing association that employs 300 staff.

A typical day

Rik arrives at work at about 8.30 a.m. each morning and generally works until 5 p.m. or 5.30 p.m. Rik's normal working hours range from 35 to 40 per week. Every day is different, depending on the tasks that need to take priority. Generally, though, the role requires Rik to support HR Advisors with the day-to-day operations of the HR function. These operations might include compiling and updating employee records, processing documentation and preparing reports related to staffing (such as resourcing, training, grievances and performance evaluations), coordinating HR projects (such as arranging meetings, booking training venues and administering surveys) and assisting with payroll preparation.

Rik really enjoys working with people and is great at organizing and problem-solving, which supports the efficiency of the team. He has developed effective skills in the use of databases, spreadsheets, word processing and accounts packages. As you would expect, Rik respects the need for confidentiality when dealing with personal details and is tactful, diplomatic and approachable.

Rik earns £18,000 a year; he is aware that some organizations offer more than this, some less. He hopes to move to an HR Officer/HR Advisor role in a year, after he has completed a qualification in HR. He appreciates the support of his colleagues and is increasing his skills and knowledge every day.

Case study: Shazia

Job title: HR Business Partner (described as HR Advisor in some organizations; in very large organizations both jobs may exist, with HR Business Partner being more senior)

Shazia graduated with a degree in English 10 years ago, completing a postgraduate certificate in Education immediately afterwards, with a view to training as a teacher. After qualifying,

Shazia found that teaching was not for her, although she did enjoy preparing for class and the satisfaction of helping people to learn. Shazia entered HR as a learning and development administrator, gradually taking on more responsibility as she became more experienced. She applied for a role as HR Assistant in the finance company where she worked. This provided her with valuable experience in generalist HR and she was promoted to HR Advisor 2 years later. Shazia now works for a large investment bank as an HR Business Partner.

A typical day

Shazia likes to start work early and so she arrives at around 8 a.m. each day. It is a very busy role with a considerable amount of variety. Shazia supports a business unit of 450 employees across commercial banking. She works with teams across the talent, learning and development, reward and HR operations departments to support the client group across areas such as workforce planning, process improvement and employee engagement. She works closely with senior leaders, providing coaching and guidance in support of all aspects of the employee lifecycle, with a particular emphasis on complex employee-relations issues, succession planning, leadership development plans and recruitment strategy.

Shazia is naturally driven and enjoys working autonomously, which is helpful because she is required to manage an employee-relations caseload from inception to resolution. She is also an effective communicator, working on projects and change programmes that require her to liaise with stakeholders across the business. She completed her level 5 CIPD diploma a few years ago and is now considering undertaking level 7. Shazia feels that this will prepare her well for her next role, perhaps as an HR Manager or Head of HR. She currently earns £48,000 a year, which she feels is fair for the value that she brings and comparable with other HR Business Partner roles in the sector.

Case study: Buckholi

Job title: Director of HR

Buckholi graduated with a business degree 20 years ago. As she had particularly enjoyed the organizational-behaviour and people-related modules on her programme of study, she decided to pursue a career in HR. She secured a role as an HR Administrator in a design company and was sponsored by the organization to complete her CIPD level 3 certificate in HR practice. It was a small team – just Buckholi and her manager – and this allowed her to gain experience across all aspects of HR. From there, Buckholi secured an HR Advisor role with a large pharmaceutical organization, where she was able to develop her employee-relations skills working across one division of the business. It was a busy role but Buckholi enjoyed liaising with line managers and supporting them with people management. There was a considerable amount of learning to do in this post and Buckholi was thankful for her team's support and for her mentor, who was allocated to her from another division of the organization.

After 2 years, Buckholi was promoted to HR Business Partner, where she was supported by an HR Administrator. During this time, she decided that it would be a good idea to develop her HR knowledge further by undertaking the level 5 diploma in HRM. On successful completion of this qualification and together with her previous HR experience, Buckholi was successful in her application for an HR Manager role in a medium-sized insurance company. Managing a team of HR Assistants, Business Partners and specialist-skills staff, Buckholi's remit was to deliver a 3-year people strategy, ensuring that HR supported the strategic direction of the organization during a period of rapid growth. Buckholi decided it was time to study for her level 7 CIPD qualification and, although it was challenging, she found the learning useful in helping her deliver her objectives over the course of her 3 years in post. With senior-level HR experience and her postgraduate diploma in HRM, Buckholi upgraded to become a Chartered Fellow of the CIPD.

A typical day

Buckholi now works as a Director of HR in a medium-sized energy company – a role she thoroughly enjoys. This gives her the opportunity to offer real impact at the organizational level, which requires building strong relationships, understanding the external environment, and being a key player in the shaping of the organizational vision. As a member of the executive committee, Buckholi is a key advisor to the CEO and other directors on all people issues, change management, succession planning, recruitment, long-term and annual pay and reward, and major employee-relations policies. She leads the HR team, the apprenticeship and graduate training schemes, agency-supplied workers, and workforce diversity and inclusivity initiatives, and she ensures that the organization is compliant with relevant employment legislation. She currently earns £80,000 a year but knows she could earn more in a larger organization, where her remit might extend to international subsidiaries.

SPECIALIST ROLES IN HR

In addition to the generalist HR roles discussed above, there are opportunities to specialize. Some people enter their specialism directly; others might transfer after spending a few years in a generalist role. Let us explore specialist roles in the people profession in more detail.

Organization Design and Development Consultant

In this role you are likely to take a holistic view of your organization. Imagine you are hovering over the institution in a helicopter; you can see each component of the design and how departments intertwine with each other, as well as reporting lines and physical layout (including remote working). This describes organization design, where you consider how things fit together, how many people report to each manager, the layers of management and the hierarchical structure of the organization. The development side of the role can include driving performance in relation to organizational goals, leading on change management projects, and conducting evaluation exercises to assess the benefits of organizational cultural and behavioural change.

You are likely to work with stakeholders across the organization and at all levels of the hierarchy in order to assess readiness for change and to anticipate resistance, working with colleagues and managers to lead others through change. This will include the facilitation of workshops and focus groups to obtain insight and data in relation to the desired outcomes. You may also be required to line-manage multidisciplinary teams and business analysts delivering change projects.

This role requires previous experience of organization design and change management and may be suitable for generalist HR professionals wishing to specialize or perhaps for a learning and development manager wishing to advance in organizational design and development.

The actual nature of the role varies according to sector and will probably only be present in a large organization. Typically, organizations will be seeking the following knowledge, experience and skills:

- knowledge and demonstrable experience of organization design in a complex organization;

- a demonstrable human-/person-centric approach to organization design;
- change-management experience;
- experience of driving or leading key projects and delivering successful outcomes efficiently and effectively;
- excellent analytical skills and aptitude for data;
- evidence of continuously developing yourself and others and of creating an environment of continuous learning and improvement;
- a 'can-do' style of working and a proactive and curious mindset;
- excellent relationship management skills with the ability to manage conflicting stakeholder views and interests to deliver successful outcomes;
- a high level of written and oral communication skills and the ability to influence and negotiate effectively, persuasively and sensitively; and
- a relevant professional qualification.

Head of Learning & Development/ Learning & Development Manager

Learning and development professionals often specialize from the start of their career, but it is also possible to move across horizontally from an HR generalist position. Here you must have a strong understanding of how learning and development aligns with the delivery of organizational goals and objectives so you can support the delivery of the strategy. The learning and development team are generally responsible for identifying skills gaps, comparing people's capabilities with the business strategy and designing and developing learning solutions. This may include using digital learning to support delivery of organizational goals. This is a very people-focused role and specialists will work closely with stakeholders on a range of projects. You will need to manage the learning and development budget to ensure efficient and effective use of resources, and you will be responsible for evaluating initiatives in terms of return on investment. As a department head or learning and development manager you will probably be managing a team of specialists.

The actual nature of the role will vary according to the sector and the size of the organization, but organizations will typically be seeking the following knowledge, experience and skills:

- the ability to think strategically to support the delivery of the corporate strategy within a changing environment;
- a positive, inclusive and collegial leadership style, and the ability to inspire, motivate and develop others to achieve results;
- expert-level knowledge of the full learning cycle, including learning needs analysis and return on investment;
- the ability to work as an effective member of the management team in shaping, supporting and driving forward the learning and development plan;
- experience of budget and financial management;
- effective project management skills;
- excellent stakeholder management skills;
- the ability to diagnose capability gaps and identify innovative and creative learning interventions;
- excellent influencing and negotiation skills;
- effective leadership skills, such as in providing direction to high-level learning and development initiatives, and the ability to direct and develop a team and to deliver at pace;
- a relevant professional qualification; and
- e-learning and digital learning expertise is desirable.

Reward Business Partner/Analyst/Specialist

In this role you will be responsible for providing specialist reward expertise to your organization. This requires a continuous assessment of the market competitiveness of the organization's reward strategy so that it is effective in attracting, motivating and retaining talent. An essential part of the role is keeping up to date with best practices and providing guidance to the senior management team on the organization's reward package. It will be helpful to have some experience of reward management and recognition practices such as pay models, job evaluation frameworks and benchmarking tools. You will spend quite a bit of your time advising on pay and reward issues and influencing senior managers and other stakeholders in relation to good practice and market values.

You will likely have experience in generalist HR before specializing in reward, or you may transfer from a finance background.

The actual nature of the role will vary according to the sector and will more than likely be seen in a large organization. Typically, organizations will be seeking the following knowledge, experience and skills:

- excellent knowledge of reward and recognition practices including pay models, job evaluation frameworks and benchmarking tools;
- significant experience of advising on a full range of pay and reward issues;
- demonstrable experience of working with and influencing senior managers and other stakeholders on reward and recognition;
- very strong analytical skills, as well as proficiency in using Microsoft Excel and HR systems;
- a relevant degree, or equivalent experience, with a professional qualification preferred;
- excellent interpersonal and relationship management skills, with a consulting mentality, and the ability to coordinate and integrate ideas and solutions across teams;
- numeracy and computer literacy;

- good communication skills, English language fluency, with the ability to convey complex information in a simple and engaging way;
- effective problem-solving skills and the ability to manage conflicting priorities within tight deadlines, prioritizing work effectively; and
- the ability to work autonomously and to exercise sound judgement.

HR Data Business Analyst/HR Data Manager

This role focuses on the collection and analysis of data to improve people-data reporting provision across a business. In this specialism you will deliver information to line managers and business stakeholders to support decision making. The data analyst role moves the HR profession from a function that responds to ad hoc data reporting to being a sophisticated business partner capable of delivering a trend-focused approach. In this role you will work with internal stakeholders within the HR function to maximize the effectiveness of key strategic and operational projects across reward, talent, engagement and resourcing, organizational design, HR business partnering and HR operations. You will be the main point of contact for all people analytics in the business, ensuring data accuracy of the HR information system to track total people costs, including pensions and benefits. You will also provide headcount data to predict staffing levels and costs. You will need to ensure that all data are stored and shared in a safe way, adhering to the General Data Protection Regulation. You may progress from HR Assistant to HR Data Analyst, or you may transfer from a business analyst role.

The actual nature of the role will vary according to the sector and will more than likely be seen in a large organization. Organizations will typically be seeking the following knowledge, experience and skills:

- experience of using reporting tools for the extraction and manipulation of data;
- experience of using specialist HR information systems;
- analytical and numeracy skills, with keen attention to detail;
- the ability to work with stakeholders across the business and to respond effectively to requests;
- an approachable, diplomatic, discrete and thoughtful personality, with a drive to succeed;
- the ability to provide business intelligence and management information to a wide range of stakeholders;
- the ability to use data to identify internal and external trends based on benchmarking information;
- proficiency in developing a suite of reports that can be accessed via self-service;
- knowledge of process analysis and continuous improvement tools (and mindset), e.g. Lean, Six Sigma; and
- knowledge of HR functions and products/services, with experience of working in an HR function.

Talent Acquisition Manager

This specialist role is about ensuring that an organization has the right people in the right place at the right time. In this role you will manage all aspects of recruitment, including onboarding and ongoing HR support for candidates and colleagues, and you will ensure that all processes are fair and inclusive. In larger organizations you will look after hires both internally and externally. You will be responsible for aligning recruitment processes with the employer brand, creating an employee value proposition to ensure that the organizational values and behaviours are fully embedded into all aspect of the recruitment cycle. This is generally a fast-paced role in which you are required to liaise with a wide range of senior stakeholders to understand their workforce requirements on a short-, medium- and long-term basis. You may be able to identify opportunities for improving talent sourcing and assessment capability through technology.

Other specialist roles that align with this speciality include Talent Attraction Specialist and employer brand positions, which are more likely to be seen in large organizations. You may progress from an HR Assistant to a talent acquisition role, or you may transfer from a recruiter role.

The actual nature of the role will vary according to the sector. In large organizations this will be a specialist role; in smaller organizations this role may form part of a generalist HR role. Organizations will typically be seeking the following knowledge, experience and skills:

- experience of leading a high-performing talent acquisition team;
- a demonstrable ability to build happy, empowered, efficient and customer-focused services;
- some familiarity with overseas recruitment and immigration processes, depending on the organization;
- in-depth knowledge of selection assessment tools;
- commitment to the importance of equality, diversity and inclusion throughout the candidate and employee experience;
- experience of managing budgets and the ability to achieve great results to a budget;
- the ability to negotiate with and influence a wide range of stakeholders;
- proven project management skills;
- an analytical and inquisitive mindset and the ability to produce and monitor meaningful key performance indicators (KPIs); and
- a keen understanding of modern recruitment technologies and of how best to leverage their capabilities.

Employee Engagement Manager/Internal Communication
In this role you will be developing and delivering an organization's internal communication strategy and planning a calendar activity to increase levels of employee engagement. This might involve leading on the development and implementation of engagement platforms and providing expert advice to senior stakeholders on critical decisions and messages that affect employees. A key part of the role will be about driving the creation of the employee brand. This will require a consistent approach to internal communication channels, including the intranet, employee newsletters and email announcements. You will work closely with the HR team and other stakeholders on the employee engagement strategy, and you will oversee the measurement of internal communication engagement activity and link this to KPIs.

You may progress from an HR or learning and development assistant role to an employee engagement or internal communication role, or you might transfer from a marketing role, a public relations role or another related role. Organizations will typically be seeking the following knowledge, experience and skills:

- the ability to build and manage positive relationships with senior stakeholders;
- experience of project management and of developing systems to improve efficiency
- an understanding of how to manage change;
- the ability to write compelling copy and to craft messages for an internal audience;
- experience of working independently and balancing multiple projects;
- the ability to understand and evaluate the benefits of current digital communications and technology, with a commitment to a 'digital first' approach;

- experience of working in an internal communications department;
- knowledge and understanding of good-practice employee-engagement theory;
- familiarity with medium- to large-sized organizations and matrixed structures/reporting lines; and
- experience of setting up and introducing new employee engagement platforms (e.g. Microsoft Teams, Workplace from Facebook, Slack).

THE IMPACT OF ORGANIZATION SIZE AND SECTOR

The exact nature of job roles will differ according to whether the organization is in the private sector (owned by individuals), the public sector (owned by government) or the third sector (owned and run voluntarily by trustees).

In the private sector the focus is profit. People management roles may exist in all sizes of organization: partnerships (where two or more people own the organization), SMEs (small to medium sized enterprises; typically those that employ fewer than 250 people) and large multinational organizations that are producing and selling goods/services across several countries.

The public sector refers to any organization that is run by (central or local) government as well as state-run healthcare services, schools and emergency services. Organizations of varying types and sizes exist in this sector.

The third sector refers to the not-for-profit or voluntary sectors, which operate in the space between the private and public sectors. They are typically independent of government and are values driven, i.e. focused on social goals rather than profit, reinvesting surplus profit into pursuing organizational goals.

The variety of people management roles will likely depend on the size of the organization. A small company of fewer than 50 employees may only require one stand-alone people professional, whereas a large organization employing thousands will have a larger people function with the opportunity to specialize.

The nature of job roles will differ depending on the sector, size and purpose of the organization. For example, people professionals working in the private sector are likely to be outcomes driven and commercially focused. In the public sector there tends to be more ambiguity, with multiple stakeholders involved in decision making. Decision making tends to be faster paced in the private sector. In the public sector pay tends to be fixed and people managers need to focus on how to motivate people beyond monetary considerations. In the private sector there is much more opportunity for creative reward packages. In the private sector people policies such as learning and development and well-being need to be in alignment with the brand.

Reporting lines will naturally vary according to the size of an organization. In small organizations the people professional is likely to report directly to the CEO. Larger organizations are more likely to have functional structures in place. People professionals might find that they have dual reporting lines in a large matrix structure, meaning that they are accountable not only to the function as a whole but also perhaps to a specific project or division.

Let us now take a look at some examples of how HR roles might differ in organizations of different sizes operating across the three sectors.

HR in an SME in the third sector

Tom is an operations manager at a theatre. Since the team is fairly small, with no HR department, his role requires him to oversee all elements of HR for the organization, as well as taking on other secretarial and charity governance duties. Here is what Tom has to say about his job:

> My career has been quite varied so far. I've worked as an events manager, sales executive, receptionist and finance assistant. I really enjoy the variety of my current role and feel that this is the first time in 20 years that I can start focussing on my work and developing my career. I have just enrolled [in] the level 3 diploma in HRM at my local college to support my career in HR.

HR in an SME in the private sector

Talia completed her law degree in 2018 and has been working as an HR administrator ever since. Here is what she says about her role:

> My first role was within a local law firm, which heavily focused on onboarding, induction and employee benefits. I moved to my new role in a construction company a few months ago and it has already given me much more responsibility and exposure to HR. I'm currently working on managing immigration for the whole company, the employee benefits platform, absence review and writing policies and guidance for managers.

HR in a large organization in the private sector

Mia works as an HR and training assistant for a wealth management company. Mia says:

> My role is a generalist one and I get involved with screening new recruits, well-being initiatives and I'm currently undertaking research for a new HR system. I started work as a compliance administrator in a hospital before joining my current organization. My company sponsored me to complete the level 3 diploma in HR

practice last year and this has been really helpful in providing some helpful underpinning theory in my current role.

HR in a medium-sized organization in the public sector

Runha, an HR and business advisor at a council with 750 staff, has this to say about her job:

> My role covers all elements of HR, with a particular focus on employee relations and organizational change. I work with a great team. My early career was in administration, which led to roles in facilities management at other councils, and I also spent a few years in the leisure industry. I had a career break when I had my daughter and then I took a role in my local school as [an] HR Administrator. This was an amazing turning point for me as it gave me the experience to … gain skills and knowledge to support me in my current role.

HR in a medium-sized organization in the private sector

Zarina currently works as an HR Advisor at a food manufacturing company, which specializes in the production of luxury dog food. She says:

> I find this industry very interesting and enjoy the mixture of different personalities that comes from supporting operations, technical and support staff. My role consists of predominantly employee relations, including absence management, performance management and employee engagement. However, as a generalist I tend to support my colleagues wherever needed.
>
> I also thoroughly enjoy project work and I have just implemented a new HR system, which has saved the department and the business considerable time due to a reduction in manual administration.

> I have worked in my present organization for the past 3 years. Prior to this, I was an HR Advisor at an insurance company and, before this, an HR Administrator at a hospice. I completed my CIPD level 5 diploma a few years ago and I am now just about to start my level 7 diploma. I am very ambitious and therefore hoping to progress into an HR Business Partner/Manager role with a more strategic focus soon. I am keen to become an HR Consultant at some point in the future.

HR in a medium-sized organization in the third sector

Gayshini currently works as a people assistant at a housing group based in London. Here is what she has to say about her role:

> I started my career in HR 3 years [ago], straight from sixth form college. I was fortunate to be recruited onto [an] HR apprenticeship at my current employer and I am now in the process of my promotion to people officer! The organization has given me exposure to many different aspects of HR in my short career. I have been given opportunities to deliver aspects of our people strategy, been coached through various high-level ER [employee relations] cases and I also support internal communications. I am now exploring the level 7 CIPD diploma as I am keen to advance to HR Business Partner within the next few years.

HOW MUCH CAN YOU EXPECT TO GET PAID?

Salaries vary according to both the nature and the seniority of HR roles. Reed produced a 'Salary Guide' that shows pay across both generalist and specialist HR roles for 2021.[7] Tables 2 and 3 show average salary ranges for the London region. Although regional variations might account for differences of up to £15,000, these data provide benchmarks for different HR roles.

Table 2 Generalist HR role salaries.

	Lower	Average	Upper
HR Director	£74,800	£84,100	£93,300
HR Manager	£51,800	£57,100	£62,400
HR Business Partner	£53,300	£58,000	£62,700
HR Advisor	£34,900	£37,500	£40,100
HR Administrator	£25,100	£26,800	£28,400
HR Analyst	£42,000	£46,500	£50,900

Table 3 Specialist HR role salaries.

	Lower	Average	Upper
Reward Manager	£64,600	£70,600	£76,500
HR Project Manager	£55,300	£61,100	£66,900
Organizational Development Specialist	£55,300	£59,500	£63,500
Employee Relations Manager	£53,900	£59,400	£64,700
Operations Manager	£50,700	£54,900	£59,100
Learning and Development Manager	£54,600	£59,200	£63,800
Recruitment Manager	£43,400	£52,400	£63,800
Recruitment Officer	£30,200	£31,900	£33,500

The US Bureau of Labor Statistics identified the median annual wage for HR specialists as $63,490 in May 2020, with the lowest-paid decile earning $37,710 and the highest-paid decile earning $109,350.[8] The median annual wages for human resources specialists in the industries in which they worked are shown in table 4.

The average pay for HR Managers in the US in 2020 was $121,220 per year, or $58.28 per hour. The median annual wages for HR Managers in the industries in which they worked are shown in table 5.

IS HR RIGHT FOR YOU?

Having reviewed both the generalist and specialist roles in HR, you will have noticed that the required skills and knowledge across the

Table 4 Median annual wages in the US, by sector.

Professional, scientific and technical services	$71,960
Government	$70,410
Manufacturing	$66,980
Employment services	$54,920
Healthcare and social assistance	$54,170

Table 5 Median annual wages for HR Managers in the US, by sector.

Professional, scientific and technical services	$138,030
Management of companies and enterprises	$133,860
Manufacturing	$119,880
Government	$105,830
Healthcare and social assistance	$101,990

Data from *Occupational Outlook Handbook*, Bureau of Labor Statistics, US Department of Labor (www.bls.gov/ooh/management/human-resources-managers.htm).

Table 6 Consider the following questions and rate yourself with a tick against the most appropriate rank: low, medium or high.

	Low	Medium	High
Am I business focused?			
Do I enjoying looking ahead, planning and being a strategic thinker?			
Do I enjoy solving problems?			
Do I enjoy working with people?			
Do I enjoy working with data and research?			
Can I maintain confidentiality?			
Am I approachable?			

areas is quite broad. There are some core areas that can be transferred to most of the roles, though. Why not review your preferences using table 6? This might help you decide if HR is for you.

SUMMARY

In this chapter we have reviewed both generalist and specialist roles in HR and the ways in which these positions might differ across organizations of varying sizes and operating in different sectors. We have established that, although many people do progress vertically through the ranks of HR to senior positions, others transfer into the profession after gaining experience in other roles. Through the case study examples we have seen how the profession and its advancement opportunities are open to both graduates and non-graduates. Many HR professionals undertake professional qualifications to support their progression, and these can be undertaken at any age based on one's experience.

Chapter 3

HR PROFESSIONAL BODIES

PROFESSIONAL BODIES ARE ASSOCIATIONS AND societies with individual members that practise a profession or occupation. These organizations oversee the knowledge, skills, conduct and practices required to operate successfully in that profession. A professional body supports individuals with the advancement of their careers, defining specific skills, experience and academic principles that will aid their development. The professional body facilitates solutions to the professional needs and interests of its members, and it provides access to member benefits that are specific to the profession.

In the UK alone there are more than eighty chartered professional institutions, covering professions in finance, engineering, leadership and management, health, law, journalism and people management, and there are reportedly 92,000 trade and professional bodies in the US. There are many membership organizations that support people management professionals in all parts of the world. In the US alone there are dozens of national groups spanning all HR areas and roles. These include bodies with a broad scope and ones with a narrower focus within the field. Some examples are the Society for Human Resource Management (the largest association dedicated to global HR), the Association for Talent Development (which focuses on organizational development and/or learning and development), the Human Capital Institute (focusing on talent management), World at

Work (focusing on total rewards), the American Payroll Association (focusing on payroll administration and practice) and the Society for Industrial and Organizational Psychology (for those with a psychology interest).

Many countries have their own professional associations that keep their members informed, interconnected and supported. Some examples are the South African Board of People Practices, the Hong Kong Institute of Human Resource Management, the Canadian Human Resources Management Association, the Human Resources Society in Nepal, the Institute of Human Resource Management Practitioners in Ghana, the Chartered Institute of Human Resources Management in Nigeria, the Australian HR Institute, the Maldives Association of Human Resource Professionals, and, of course, the CIPD in the UK.

In this chapter we will explore and compare the two biggest HR professional bodies: the Society for Human Resource Management (SHRM)[9] in the US and the Chartered Institute of Personnel and Development (CIPD)[10] in the UK. We will also look at three smaller professional bodies: namely, the Singapore Human Resources Institute (SHRI),[11] the Institute of Human Resource Management Practitioners (IHRMP)[12] in Ghana and the Australian HR Institute (AHRI).[13] We will assess the benefits of and requirements for membership and the progression routes, accreditation and competency-based frameworks for each organization in turn.

HR PROFESSIONAL BODIES

Society for Human Resource Management

The SHRM was established in 1948 and is now the largest people management professional body in the world, with more than 300,000 members in 165 countries. Equity, diversity and inclusion are at the heart of their vision for building a better workforce.

Membership

Becoming a member of the SHRM gives you access to compliance resources, tools and samples to support people professionals in their everyday roles. Thousands of customizable templates are available, for job descriptions, policies, toolkits, forms and so on. There is also an 'Ask the advisor' facility so that people professionals can get advice on key HR-related questions. The SHRM also offers discounts on competency-based education programmes, in the form of events, seminars and e-learning, along with professional-development tools to support progression, such as presentations, webcasts and career resources. Professional qualifications provide the basis for both new and experienced individuals to accelerate their careers through accredited behavioural competency-based certification (see chapter 4). There are also a wide range of opportunities for building one's networks and a great deal of support for peer-to-peer interaction, including opportunities to connect with executives and thought leaders in the field.

Members are able to join one of five categories: professional, global, student, executive and enterprise. The professional membership is geared towards those working in HR on a day-to-day basis, with benefits including access to best practice, resources, tools and HR solutions. Global membership provides access to global best practice, trends, research, HR metrics calculators, sample policies, job descriptions, interview questions and also an online community. The student category is aimed at those looking for scholarships, career advice, conferences, HR news, reports and networking opportunities. Executive network membership is reserved for those with 10–15 years of progressive HR and/or leadership experience, including strategic responsibility, or for those with an advanced degree in business/management. The SHRM enterprise category is the member offer relevant to organizations. It provides a suite of customizable assessment tools, industry-specific employee training, competency development and support to maximize workplace competitiveness.

In addition to legal and compliance resources, interactive tools, employee handbooks, a vendor directory and networking opportunities, membership provides access to the latest updates on HR news, public policy and research. The society's *HR Magazine* provides in-depth analysis of HR trends and issues, allowing people professionals to stay up to date with the rapidly transforming workplace. Resources also include SHRM Benchmarking Services, which provide benchmarking reports on topics such as human capital, employee benefits, healthcare, paid leave and talent acquisition. In partnership with the website Salary.com, the SHRM provides compensation data for over 15,000 job titles across 225 industries to support people professionals with compiling compensation analysis data. Other tools offered include the SHRM Talent Assessment Center, which provides access to a suite of online talent assessments, and the Employee Engagement Suite, which includes access to the SHRM's employee engagement survey, their new hire survey, their exit survey and their 360-degree feedback tool.

The SHRM is also one of the most popular areas to find HR jobs, with hundreds of new vacancies posted each month, covering every discipline in the people profession. Many HR professionals post their resumé/CV on the site, and this provides employers with a searchable database of highly qualified HR candidates.

As a career partner, the SHRM provides a comprehensive set of resources to support professional development in a variety of learning formats, including instructor-led programmes (in person and online), e-learning self-paced courses and on-site in-company training. The SHRM also has a dedicated learning system for the 'Certified Professional' and 'Senior Certified Professional' exams (see chapter 4). A full programme of events is delivered centrally and regionally through the local chapter network, which consists of 575 affiliated chapters (equivalent to branches in the UK) promoting opportunities for local networking.

The SHRM body of competency and knowledge model

The competency model was designed in collaboration with HR professionals, corporations and universities from thirty-three countries. The model consists of nine competencies, including eight behavioural competencies and one technical one, all of which are required in any HR role regardless of the size or sector of the organization. The model provides the key competencies required throughout the HR lifecycle, and people professionals can use it to guide their career development. The SHRM divides careers into four levels: early level, mid level, senior level and executive level. At the early level, little to no HR experience is required and work is likely to be carried out at a transactional level, with the postholder supporting other functions. At the mid level, the postholder has moderate experience and leads or supports operational functions, including small to medium-sized projects, focusing on the implementation of the HR plan. At the senior level, the postholder is likely to have significant experience, working at a strategic level as a leader in the organization, or perhaps as an HR consultant. At the executive level, the HR professional is likely to be one of the most senior leaders in HR, holding the top HR job in their organization or even a Vice President role.

The SHRM competency model consists of eight behavioural competencies grouped into three clusters, under the headings leadership, interpersonal and business.

Leadership

Leadership and navigation. This competency encompasses the 'knowledge, skills, abilities and other characteristics' (KSAOs) needed to navigate an organization and to accomplish HR goals; to create a compelling vision and mission for HR that aligns with the strategic direction and culture of the organization; to lead and promote organizational change; to manage the implementation and execution of HR initiatives; and to promote the role of HR as a key business partner.

Ethical practice. This competency encompasses the KSAOs needed to maintain high levels of personal and professional integrity, and to act as an ethical agent who promotes core values, integrity and accountability throughout the organization.

Interpersonal

Relationship management. This competency encompasses the KSAOs needed to create and maintain a network of professional contacts within and outside the organization; to build and maintain relationships; to work as an effective member of a team; and to manage conflict while supporting the organization.

Communication. This encompasses the KSAOs needed to effectively craft and deliver concise and informative communications; to listen to and address the concerns of others; and to transfer and translate information from one level or unit of an organization to another.

Global and cultural effectiveness. This encompasses the KSAOs needed to value and consider the perspectives and backgrounds of all parties; to interact with others in a global context; and to promote a diverse and inclusive workplace.

Business

Business acumen. This competency encompasses the KSAOs needed to understand the organization's operations, functions and external environment, and to apply business tools and analyses that not only inform HR initiatives and operations but are also consistent with the overall strategic direction of the organization.

Consultation. This encompasses the KSAOs needed to work with organizational stakeholders in evaluating business challenges and identifying opportunities for the design, implementation and evaluation of change initiatives. The KSAOs in this competency are also needed to build ongoing support for HR solutions that meet changing customer and business needs.

Critical evaluation. This encompasses the KSAOs needed to collect and analyse qualitative and quantitative data, and to interpret and promote findings that evaluate HR initiatives and inform business decisions and recommendations.

Technical

In addition to the behavioural competencies, the SHRM also outlines the need for one technical competency (HR expertise), which is defined as the principles, practices and functions of effective people management. The SHRM divides this into three knowledge domains – under the headings people, organization and workplace – that cover fifteen functional areas (as described in table 7 overleaf).

Technical HR competencies (what you know) and behavioural competencies (how you apply what you know) emphasize the integrated roles that contribute to effective people practice. The framework provides clarity and guidance to support career planning and future progression.

Now let us review the second largest global HR professional body.

Chartered Institute of Personnel and Development

The CIPD was established in 1913 and is now the professional body of choice for its 150,000 worldwide members. The CIPD exists to champion better work and working lives for a fairer and more prosperous society. It achieves this by influencing policy and practices in order to convince policymakers to put people first in decisions about work. They have established an internationally recognized

Table 7 Organizing framework of the technical-competency knowledge domains (HR expertise).

Domain	Functional areas
People	HR strategic planning
	Talent acquisition
	Employee engagement and retention
	Learning and development
	Total rewards
Organization	Structure of the HR function
	Organizational effectiveness and development
	Workplace management
	Employee and labour relations
	Technology management
Workplace	HR in the global context
	Diversity and inclusion
	Risk management
	Corporate social responsibility
	US employment law and regulations

gold standard for HR and people development, ensuring that the profession is trusted and valued.

Membership

CIPD membership benefits focus on three core areas: supporting people professionals in their day-to-day role; acting as a career partner by offering a range of resources to support career development; and providing opportunities for networking through the CIPD online community, the institute's fifty-two local branch networks and various volunteering opportunities.

Local branches are run by people professionals who volunteer their spare time, skills and experience to provide a series of events and activities in support of CIPD members, non-members and students. Getting involved with your local CIPD branch is an excellent way to network, learn and contribute to the professional body. As a committee member in my local branch I have delivered and facilitated a number of sessions on employment law, ethical decision making and leadership, and I find that it is a great way to benchmark and share good practice while also building a sound network of expert colleagues.

There are a number of resources to support people professionals in their roles, keeping them informed and up to date. The institute's Knowledge Hub contains a wide range of fact sheets, reports and articles in addition to more than 200 business and HR/learning and development journals via the EBSCO research database. Membership also provides access to well-being helpline services, including tools, resources and support (such as employment law support), as well as to *People Management*, the CIPD magazine.

The CIPD offers a range of courses, conferences and resources to support career development and enhance professional credibility. Development is focused on four levels: foundation, associate, chartered and (at the strategic level) chartered fellow membership. These levels align with membership grades in order to reflect your level of capability, knowledge and impact in the workplace. For students there is a student member status, which helps aspiring people professionals gain CIPD professional recognition.

Foundation level is aimed at those engaged in tactical, day-to-day delivery of tasks, using information to understand their work, organization and profession. At the associate level, people professionals start contributing to thinking around work and they begin analysing information to inform choices and actions. The chartered member level requires thinking at a strategic level, where people professionals critically question information and evaluate it to make judgements and decisions. At the top of the membership grades is chartered fellow status, where work is entirely focused on thinking strategically and managing both complexity and ambiguity in order to drive change.

The HR profession map

The CIPD membership grades are aligned with the professional standards set in the profession map. The map focuses on the knowledge and behaviours needed to create value and make an impact at work. In 2018 the new CIPD profession map was launched, taking account of new specialisms, ways of working and priorities. The focus shifted from best practice to value-based decision making, ensuring that the map reflects the globalized world, that it is relevant across business contexts, that it reflects all aspects of the people profession, and that it focuses on value creation and impact.

At the very centre of the CIPD profession map is the purpose of the profession – championing better work and working lives – so that each and every people professional has a role in driving this forward. Three fundamental core elements – 'evidence based', 'outcomes driven' and 'principles led' – support this mission. 'Evidence based' refers to the evidence that informs decision making, ensuring sound professional judgements. It is about understanding impact and outcomes beyond numbers alone. 'Outcomes driven' refers to the alignment of strategic priorities and operational delivery when considering the impact that being evidence based has on work, people and professionalism, taking account of both value and risk in different contexts. 'Principles led' is underpinned by three pillars: work matters, people matters and professionalism matters.

What does it mean to be evidence based?

People professionals have a significant amount of data available to support decision making, and data analytics can support planning, reviews and benchmarks. But we can also gain information from our own experiences and conversations by asking questions, assessing risks and working with stakeholders.

Robert Bolton, a partner in KPMG's Global People and Change Centre of Excellence, believes that the whole point of evidence-based

HR is to drive greater value through the better use of the most important asset an organization has: its people. He argues that:

> If leaders are accountable for people management, then HR's time and resources can be better used architecting what the workforce of the future will look like. This architecting, or 'workforce shaping', will be anchored by predictive analytics, information flows and process automation, among other digital capabilities, to help turn workforce insight into action'[14]

In turn this will drive greater customer satisfaction, revenue, higher employee engagement and commitment, and it will ultimately build a more successful, innovative company.

Companies such as IBM and Coca-Cola have already observed the correlation between people's performance and the consumer brand through recognizing, establishing and measuring the links between employees, customers and revenue. HR professionals need to understand the business context and data findings in order to ensure that employees add value to their organization.

What does it mean to be outcomes driven?

When Dave Ulrich, a professor at the University of Michigan and a partner within the RBL group, gave a presentation at the Visier Customer Forum in 2015 he told the story of a chief HR officer who was seeking advice regarding a company their organization were considering acquiring, since it had a negative culture that was very different to their own.[15] While many HR professionals might have focused on how to solve the issue, the advice given was to ask for a $10 million reduction in price. The strategy worked and the chief HR officer saved the company $10 million.

Outcomes matter, and people professionals need to combine workforce metrics with business metrics. For example, does an increase in staff turnover lead to a decrease in sales? How does the management development programme impact on revenue? Too often HR departments are reactive – embedded in operational matters that focus on policy and processes. To make any sort of impact, an outcomes-focused model is required. The ability to define and measure expectations for customers, employees and stakeholders ensures that people professionals are talking the same language as senior leaders. Being outcomes driven is about understanding context and ensuring value for your organization, the consumers and employees.

What does it mean to be principles led?

People professionals need to see beyond rules so that decisions, actions and behaviours are led by clear principles and beliefs. The CIPD has identified three key principles as the foundation of good decision making.

(1) Work matters: it should be purposeful and should allow everyone to use their skills and talents effectively so that they can find meaning in what they do. It should also be safe and inclusive, ensuring that recognition systems are fair and support both economic and social accountability in wider society.
(2) People matter: they should have access and opportunity to work and be supported with the required development and resources. They have personal responsibility for their own work, development and behaviour. They should be treated fairly and be given a meaningful voice.
(3) Professionalism matters: people professionals should be ambassadors who are committed to continual development and value-based decisions. They are experts on people, work and change, understanding how decisions impact both organizations and society.

In August 2019, 181 of America's biggest companies supported a revision to the definition of corporate purpose so that making money for shareholders and maximizing profits were no longer listed as being the top priority. Senior executives at this round-table discussion included influential leaders such as Jeff Bezos, the founder of Amazon, Tim Cook, the CEO of Apple, and Jamie Dimon, the chairman of JP Morgan.[16] The declaration stated that there should be multiple parallel commitments to improving society, providing value to customers, investing in employees, dealing ethically with suppliers, supporting local communities and protecting the environment.

People professionals can also influence businesses through the following three key principles of making good decisions, particularly when managing significant change: core knowledge, core behaviours and specialist knowledge.

The CIPD profession map details the core knowledge, core behaviours and specialist knowledge required to be an effective people professional regardless of your role, sector or specialism. The map details what you need to know in order to be an expert on people, work and change.

Core knowledge

The core knowledge section of the profession map identifies six areas of core expertise within the people profession.

- Analytics and creating value: an understanding of analytics and its use in creating insight and measuring values.
- Digital working: an understanding of the digital environment and how to apply technology in a people context.
- Change: an understanding of how to effectively enable change.
- People practice: an understanding of the range of people practices needed to be an effective people professional.

- Culture and behaviour: an understanding of people's behaviour and creating the right organizational culture.
- Business acumen: an understanding of your organization, the commercial context and the wider world of work.

Core behaviours

Core behaviours are the ways that we think and act. The CIPD has determined that the following eight behaviours are essential to be an effective people professional.

- Commercial drive: the ability to use a commercial mindset, demonstrating drive and enabling change to create value.
- Passion for learning: curiosity and the ability to make the most of opportunities to learn, improve and innovate.
- Insights focused: the willingness to ask questions and evaluate evidence and ideas, to create insight and understand the whole.
- Situational decision making: the ability to make effective and pragmatic decisions or choices based on the specific situation or context.
- Ethical practice: a commitment to building trust by being a role model for ethical behaviour, applying principles and values consistently in decision making.
- Professional courage and influence: the courage to speak up and skilfully influence others to gain buy-in.
- Valuing people: the ability to create a shared purpose and enable people's development, voice and well-being.
- Inclusive working: ability to work and collaborate across boundaries, effectively and inclusively, to achieve positive outcomes.

Specialist knowledge

The specialist knowledge section of the profession map identifies nine areas of specialist expertise within the people profession across human resources, learning and development and organization design and development.

- Organization development and design: the application of a systematic approach and behavioural science to drive organization performance.
- People analytics: the use of analytics to inform an organization's decision making.
- Resourcing: the ability to identify, attract and assess people to get the right employees for the organization.
- Reward: the creation of remuneration and benefits approaches that are aligned with current and future organization needs and market conditions.
- Talent management: the maximization of potential through talent identification, engagement and planning.
- Employee experience: the adoption of a holistic approach around engagement and well-being that enables workers to have a voice and become the best they can be.
- Employee relations: the ability to manage the relationship between an organization and its people through transparent practices and relevant law.
- Diversity and inclusion: the creation of an inclusive culture where individuals can thrive.
- Learning and development: the ability to ensure that workers have the knowledge, skills and experience to fulfil individual and organizational needs and ambitions.

The profession map provides new areas of focus for people professionals to effectively equip themselves with the skills, knowledge and expertise (with an emphasis on analytics) to create value. In chapter 4 we will explore how the revised CIPD qualifications align with the profession map.

Singapore Human Resources Institute

The SHRI was created as the Singapore Institute of Personnel Management in 1965 with thirty-four members. In August 1984 an academic board was set up to oversee the programme for their diploma in HR management. In 1993 the institute changed its name to the Singapore Human Resources Institute, and in 1994 members of the Singapore Industrial Relations Society were absorbed into the institute. In 1998 the institute adopted its present form.

The SHRI's vision is to be the leading HR authority in Singapore, championing human capital excellence by advocating HR best practices, connecting a community of HR professionals and enhancing the HR profession.

The SHRI provides a range of events and membership services to support lifelong learning, discussion exchanges and networking. These include the following.

SHRI corporate learning and consultancy

SHRI Corporation PTE Ltd is the training and consultancy arm of the institute, offering a wide range of courses in, for example, employment compliance, employee relations, compensation and rewards, organization development, learning and career development, managing change, performance management, employee engagement and strategy creation. Programmes can be customized to suit organization requirements. A range of HR and consultancy services are also available on a project or retainer basis.

Events

The SHRI organizes a wide range of events and activities including a number of annual events to help share good practice, to update members' knowledge and to provide opportunities for networking. The Singapore HR Awards are now fully established, having advanced and recognized human capital for the past 15 years.

SHRI Academy

The SHRI Academy offers lifelong learning opportunities and academic programmes, from basic certificates to masters-degree level. They also have joint programmes with the CIPD to expand international provision of HR education. In addition, the SHRI Academy runs a number of short courses accredited by the Institute for Human Resource Professionals, which provide certification to enhance the competencies of HR professionals, plus developmental and professional pathways.

Membership

The SHRI provides many levels of membership to HR and business professionals, including both individual and corporate membership.

Individual membership is available to students or HR youth leaders who are studying on a full-time or part-time basis as undergraduates in HR management and/or development at the SHRI. Associate membership is designed for any individual engaged in HR management or development in an executive, academic or advisory capacity that is approved by the SHRI council.

Professional membership is designed for those with at least 3 years of approved experience in the subject area along with successful completion of the institute's prescribed examination (unless they are exempt based on knowledge, experience and their application to the council). Fellowship is conferred on those who have achieved eminence in the practice of HR management and development and/or those who have contributed to the body of knowledge relating to the subject. An honorary life membership is also available and is bestowed on those who have demonstrated distinguished service to the institute and/or the community.

Corporate membership is available to organizations that wish to take advantage of the events, resources, services and networking available through the institute.

The Institute for Human Resource Professionals (IHRP) is the Singaporean HR professional certification body that provides accreditation for the SHRI. It was set up by the Ministry of Manpower, the National Trades Union Congress and the Singapore National Employers Federation. The IHRP is the only HR professional body in Singapore authorized to implement the national HR credentials, known as IHRP certification (see chapter 4).

Institute of Human Resource Management Practitioners

The IHRMP was established in 1978 as the Ghana Institute of Personnel Management and it registered as a professional body in 1981. It subsequently became dormant for a few years before being relaunched in 1995 with the following remit.

- Formulate professional standards to guide the conduct and performance of HR professionals in Ghana.
- Provide a forum for regular interactions among HR professionals.
- Provide a forum for continuing education for HR practitioners.
- Provide the opportunity and the environment for individuals who aspire to become practitioners to acquire professional training in order to add value to their organizations.

The IHRMP brings together HR practitioners across the Ghanaian economy in its mission 'to advance the practice of human resource management in Ghana'; its vision is 'to become a reputable professional body recognized locally and internationally'. The IHRMP offers HR management consultancy and training to share good practice and provide opportunities for continuing professional development.

In recognition of the changing nature of the HR function, the IHRMP designed and launched its professional certification programme (PCP) in 2002. Structured as four levels, the programme balances a theoretical base with a professional orientation at the higher levels.

Membership

Membership depends on one's level of experience and training in HR management. The IHRMP offers the following six categories of membership.

- Affiliate: designed as a non-professional grade and open to both students and those working in other professions connected to the institute (or those working in HR who do not meet the entry requirements for other grades).
- Student: available to individuals working towards the IHRMP's PCP.
- Associate: available to those who pass the IHRMP's final examination.
- Full: for members with sufficient work experience as HR professionals.
- Fellow: for those who have made a significant contribution to the IHRMP.
- Corporate: corporate membership is also available to support organizations that wish to engage in consultancy projects, networking and continuous learning programmes.

The PCP is designed to provide professional certification for practising HR professionals and also to provide training for polytechnic and university graduates who intend to go on to practise HR within organizations. Through assessing those with the relevant HR work experience it is possible to become a certified HR practitioner.

HR standards are protected through compliance with HR regulations including labour regulations, the Labour Act, the Alternative

Dispute Regulation Act, National Labour Commission Regulations, the National Pensions Act and the Constitution of the Republic of Ghana.

Australian Human Resources Institute

The AHRI is the professional body for HR in Australia. It sets the industry standard, which is benchmarked against both Singapore HR certification (IHRP) and the UK CIPD standard. The AHRI has a reciprocal certification arrangement in place with the CIPD so that qualified UK professionals are recognized in Australia and vice versa. This is available via AHRI international membership. The AHRI provides a wide range of learning and development opportunities in HR, people management and business, along with networking opportunities and conferences.

The AHRI was created in 1943 as the Personnel and Industrial Welfare Officers Association. Since then the institute has taken a number of guises, from the Personnel Officers Association of Australia (1949–54) to the Institute of Personnel Management Australia (1954–92), before reaching its current form.

Membership

Membership levels for individuals are available for students or graduates, mid-level professionals, managers, academics and executive HR professionals. Organizational membership is also available to support internal teams with research, events, professional development and careers. Members benefit from the *HRM Magazine*, which contains insights, case studies and advice, and also from the AHRI:ASSIST tool, which provides access to many policy templates, studies and survey reports.

The AHRI uses a 'Model of Excellence' to represent the required HR behaviours, knowledge and capabilities expected by both peers and leaders.

AHRI behaviours consist of what HR practitioners should do and what their peers expect of them in terms of their behaviours and capabilities.

- Critical and enquiring thinker: I ask challenging and critical questions, analysing data and situations to provide advice and make decisions.
- Solutions driven: I am focused on achieving business objectives through workable, best-fit solutions that fit the organization's operating environment.
- Future oriented: I am open to new ideas and learning and development, applying new and emerging technology solutions.
- Influencer: I have the capacity to develop relationships and exercise influence on others to affect actions, opinions and behaviours.
- Courageous: I challenge the status quo and I am resilient and assertive, with the necessary authority to negotiate outcomes as required.
- Understanding and caring: I demonstrate emotionally intelligent behaviour and empathize with the varied perspectives of different stakeholders in different situations.
- Collaborative: I can consult and foster productive relationships with key decision makers to support decision making.
- Credible: I am a trustworthy, ethical, personally credible person who operates with integrity and provides consistent advice.
- Resolver of issues: I bring stakeholders and teams together to deliver timely outcomes.
- Professional: I lead by example, acting appropriately according to the situation and promoting fairness and equity.

AHRI competencies are divided into what HR practitioners know in the 'I know' category.

- Business driven: I understand the organizational context and objectives.
- Expert practitioner: I can build, maintain and apply HR knowledge.
- Strategic architect: I contribute to organizational strategy and translate it into HR strategy.
- Ethical and credible activist: I influence through providing valued insights, which results in the achievement of individual and organizational objectives.

AHRI competencies are divided into what HR practitioners do in the 'I do' category.

- Workforce and workplace designer: I design a workplace that sustains a capable workforce.
- Stakeholder mentor and coach: I build and foster relationships and partnerships with key stakeholders in order to ensure organizational capability.
- Culture and change leader: I foster a productive and sustainable organizational culture.

WHY SHOULD YOU BELONG TO A PROFESSIONAL BODY?

The benefits of membership are outlined above and they differ according to the strengths of each professional body. In addition to networking, sharing good practice and professional advice, membership of the larger professional bodies is increasingly seen as a badge of individual credibility. Job advertisements in the US, Australia and the UK will most likely ask for membership of professional bodies, and the increasing recognition of these countries' respective professional associations means that the demand for professional recognition is likely to increase going forwards.

Belonging to a professional body is an investment of both time and money and, as with anything, you get out of it what you put in. Progressing through your professional body's qualification standards can be a useful way to benchmark your career development while also ensuring that key skills, knowledge and competencies stay up to date.

Activity

Explore the websites of the professional bodies discussed in this chapter. Consider how each might benefit you in your career. Your preferred choice of professional body will likely depend on your geographical location, your career aspirations and the strengths and membership numbers of the institution. The larger the professional body, the more influential it will be, and this is helpful in ensuring that, whatever route you take to acquire membership, your certification is internationally recognized and respected.

SUMMARY

We have reviewed five people management professional bodies of varying sizes from around the globe. A key reason for doing so was to emphasize the internationalization of the people profession and the growing recognition of HR as a key aspect of successful businesses. It is now increasingly possible to gain recognition for people management qualifications in different countries through reciprocal agreements between professional bodies. This is good news for those seeking an international career in people management.

As working practices evolve it is likely that more of us will utilize agile working to work effectively across different contexts. Membership of a professional body can provide support both in practice and in career partnering so that we manage our roles effectively for today and for tomorrow's changing workplace landscape.

Chapter 4

GETTING QUALIFIED

THIS CHAPTER INTRODUCES CERTIFICATION REQUIREMENTS across five different people management professional bodies: the Society for Human Resource Management (SHRM), the Chartered Institute of Personnel and Development (CIPD), the Singapore Human Resources Institute (SHRI), the Institute of Human Resource Management Practitioners (IHRMP) in Ghana and the Australian Human Resources Institute (AHRI). I discuss the eligibility criteria and entry points for certification based on qualifications and people management experience. By exploring the certification requirements of professional bodies across five continents we are able to learn more about the international context of people management, the similarities and contextual differences in curricula, and the ways in which our experience and qualifications in one country can be recognized elsewhere.

WHY SHOULD I GET CERTIFIED IN HR?

Professional qualifications provide support in building a career; they relate to specific skills and knowledge required in that profession. Professional qualifications are designed to train you to meet particular standards for practising HR at varying levels of seniority, as they are linked to the standards set for ethics and practice by the professional body. Therefore, professional qualifications ensure the maintenance of high standards and professional conduct. Some offer chartered status (considered a mark of professional competency and awarded by chartered bodies) and membership of the professional body as long as you meet certain levels of work experience. Getting qualified ensures that you are recognized as an expert and a leader in the people profession, and that you remain current and competitive in today's rapidly evolving economy. Being qualified thus distinguishes you from colleagues, evidencing your competency, skills and knowledge.

Employers increasingly require membership of relevant professional bodies and this is often stated in job advertisements. For example, the following advertisement for an HR Adviser at the University for the Creative Arts in the UK clearly outlines professional membership requirements:

> We are looking for a CIPD level 5 qualified and experienced HR Adviser to provide a customer-focused and high-quality HR service. The role is based at our Farnham campus, but the postholder will need to provide support to managers across all campuses, so the role requires some travel and may facilitate some homeworking.

Similarly, a recent advertisement for an HR role with Formula 1 in London states that applicants must have a CIPD qualification level 5, proven experience of working within an HR advisory role and excellent administration/organizational skills with demonstrated ability to meet deadlines.

A head of human resources vacancy for the Global Care charity on the US east coast listed the following requirements:

- over 10 years of experience in global HR leadership roles, preferably frontline customer support organizations;

- a bachelor's degree majoring in human resources management, business management, organizational development, or another related field;
- functional expertise across all general areas of HR, including organizational design, diversity and inclusion, employee experience, talent management, performance management and compensation;
- demonstrated experience leading global programmes/ initiatives with multiple stakeholders;
- strong expertise in developing solutions based on facts/data analytics;
- experience working in a fast-paced, high-performance culture in a dynamic business environment;
- exceptional consulting, coaching and facilitation skills;
- excellent communication skills, both written and verbal, as well as prioritization skills, with the ability to manage competing business and customer needs while adapting messaging appropriately for a broad range of audiences in a highly autonomous and fast-paced environment;
- human resources professional certification (e.g. SPHR, CIPD).

However, not all people management jobs require certification, and even those who were certified members of a professional body at the start of their studies may no longer be members. It is therefore not an essential requirement in some cases, and as with many professional roles, experience in the job matters most. Nevertheless, in a competitive job market it helps to have all the tools to meet the essential criteria. Therefore, although they are not mandatory, professional qualifications can help applicants stand out. This is particularly beneficial for those at the beginning of their people management career.

HOW SHOULD I GET QUALIFIED?

Professional qualifications can be studied on a full-time or part-time basis depending on the course. It helps to have some work experience in the field prior to study but professional bodies are increasingly creating entry-level routes for those without the requisite experience. The professional body is the awarding body (the body that issues qualifications and recognizes knowledge, skills and competencies following an assessment and validation procedure), which works with a number of accredited education providers to offer programmes of study. It is usually possible to study for professional qualifications through in-person sessions, distance learning, live online learning or a mixture of each through a blended programme.

The competency-based assessment route

If you have experience in people management and/or learning and development and would like to gain a qualification but you are unable to commit to a programme of study, you might consider the competency-based assessment route. This pathway allows you to draw on your previous work experience and to receive guidance on how to tailor this to the professional accreditation requirements.

Now let us review how to get qualified through different professional bodies.

Getting qualified with the Society for Human Resource Management

There are two levels at which people professionals can be certified with the SHRM: as a certified professional (CP) or as a senior certified professional (SCP).

SHRM certified professional status is aimed at HR professionals in the early or middle part of their career who implement policies and strategies, serve as a point of contact for staff and stakeholders, deliver HR services and perform at an operational level in their respective organizations. Eligibility for certified professional status varies depending on a candidate's work experience and their educational qualifications. To achieve certified professional status, candidates are required to sit a 4-hour computer-based exam that includes 160 multiple-choice questions (95 knowledge-based questions and 65 situational-judgement items). For those with less than a bachelor's degree and no former HR-related study, a minimum of 4 years' work experience is required before candidates are eligible to sit the exam. For those with some previous study in HR, 3 years' experience is required. Candidates with an HR-related bachelor's degree must have 1 year of experience; where their degree is not HR related, a candidate must have 2 years' experience. Graduates with a postgraduate degree in HR are eligible to sit the exam as long as they are currently working in the people profession. For those with a non-HR-related postgraduate degree, a minimum length of a year is required in post prior to taking the assessment.

The SHRM senior certified professional qualification is tailored to senior professionals working at a strategic level within their organization, where they are required to influence decision making, analyse performance metrics and align people management with organizational goals. To be eligible to sit the 4-hour exam, which is designed in exactly the same format as the certified professional qualification, candidates generally require more work experience in a related role. For those with less than a bachelor's degree (i.e. those working towards a bachelor's degree or who hold an associate degree, a qualifying HR certificate programme or a high school diploma) but who are following an HR-related programme of study, 6 years' HR experience is required. For those with neither a bachelor's degree nor an HR-related qualification, 7 years of working in HR is required. With a bachelor's degree, the work experience requirement is reduced to 4 years with an HR-related degree and

5 years with an unrelated programme. With a graduate degree, the amount of work experience is reduced still further: to 3 years with an HR-related degree and 4 years for a non-HR-related degree.

Assessment

The SHRM-CP and SHRM-SCP exams include two types of multiple-choice questions: stand-alone knowledge-based ones that assess a candidate's knowledge and understanding of factual information, and scenario-based situational judgement items that aim to assess a candidate's judgement, application and decision-making skills. The exams are delivered by computer over a 4-hour period that includes a break of 15 minutes if desired.

Mode of delivery

The SHRM has a dedicated learning resource that supports learners to prepare for certification through the application of HR knowledge and competencies to real-life situations. Self-study and instructor-led programmes are available depending on learner preferences. The programme starts with a 160-question assessment designed to test knowledge and identify gaps. The resource then guides candidates through the most relevant bite-sized topics based on their knowledge gaps. There are more than 2,000 practice questions, flashcards and videos to apply and reinforce both knowledge and competencies prior to working through a series of tips on exam technique.

The SHRM learning system consists of four learning modules that are constructed against the SHRM 'Body of Competence and Knowledge', as outlined in table 8.

Activity

Review your competencies according to the SHRM Body of Competence and Knowledge. Which areas do you identify as strengths? Which areas might you need to focus on?

Table 8 The SHRM's Body of Competence and Knowledge.

HR competency	People	Organization	Workplace
Business acumen	Employee engagement and retention	Employee and labour relations	Corporate social responsibility
Communication	HR strategic planning	Organizational effectiveness and development	Diversity and inclusion
Consultation	Learning and development	Structure of the HR function	HR in the global context
Critical evaluation	Talent acquisition	Technology management	Risk management
Ethical practice	Total rewards	Workforce management	US employment law and regulations (US only)
Global and cultural effectiveness			
Leadership and navigation			
Relationship management			

The competency and knowledge model helps ensure effective individual performance and the capability to deliver successful business outcomes.

Recertification is required every 3 years and professionals need to earn sixty professional development credits (PDCs) between the recertification cycle beginning and end dates in order to recertify. Recertification credits are awarded for the PDC categories 'advance your education', 'advance your profession' and/or 'advance your organization'. Further information on continuing professional development can be found in chapter 10.

Getting qualified with the CIPD

There are currently about 25,000 students studying CIPD qualifications internationally. In January 2021 the CIPD relaunched their framework, setting the international standard for people professionals. Their revised people profession map defines the knowledge, behaviours and values underpinning the profession today, providing a platform from which to advance the profession individually and collectively and to embrace the contemporary working environment. The CIPD is the only professional body in the world to offer chartered status to individual HR and learning and development professionals.

The CIPD qualification framework

Whether you are just starting a career in people management, transitioning from another career or seeking to progress, CIPD qualifications are designed to increase your knowledge and skills so you are able to make an impact in your organization, sector and profession.

There are five qualifications to choose from, ranging from foundation level to advanced:

Level 3

- Foundation Certificate in People Practice

Level 5

- Associate Diploma in People Management
- Associate Diploma in Organizational Learning and Development

Level 7

- Advanced Diploma in Strategic People Management
- Advanced Diploma in Strategic Learning and Development

CIPD qualifications are recognized globally as a standard of excellence. The qualification will also give you CIPD membership, connecting you to a network of expert people practitioners and academics. It ensures that you are connected to the most up-to-date developments in the profession on a global scale. CIPD qualifications are underpinned by the profession map discussed in chapter 3.

Let us explore the CIPD qualifications in more detail.

Foundation Certificate in People Practice

The foundation certificate is designed for those who are at the start of their journey, ready to embark on a career in people practice, or for those in a support role who are ready to advance to the next level of their career. The certificate includes the following four core units.

Business, culture and change in context

This unit explores the impact of external influences, including how the digital and commercial environment shapes businesses and culture. It also considers the importance of people's behaviour in organizational culture and the ability to manage change effectively.

Principles of analytics

People professionals make both straightforward and complex choices as they carry out their roles. This unit explores how using a diverse range of analytics and evidence is essential to situational decision making.

Core behaviours for people professionals

Focusing on ethical practice to create value, this unit considers how thinking and acting should be consistent in new and changing situations in order to promote a sense of well-being and inclusivity in one's organization.

Essentials of people practice

This module is larger than the others. It incorporates a practice-based element that introduces the fundamentals of people practice, from the employee lifecycle to policies, regulation and law. It explores subjects such as recruitment, talent management, reward and learning, and development.

Associate Diploma in People Management

To be awarded a level 5 Associate Diploma in People Management you will be required to complete a total of seven units.

The core units that you must successfully complete are

- organizational performance and culture in practice,
- evidence-based practice, and
- professional behaviours and valuing people.

The three specialist units that you must also successfully complete are

- employment relationship management,
- talent management and workforce planning, and
- reward for performance and contribution.

It is then possible to select one additional specialist unit to make up the total required credits for this qualification (forty-two credits). Learners are required to choose from the following list:

- specialist employment law;
- advances in digital learning and development;
- learning and development essentials;
- people management in an international context;
- diversity and inclusion;
- leadership and management development;
- well-being at work.

Associate Diploma in Organizational Learning and Development

To be awarded a level 5 Associate Diploma in Organizational Learning and Development you will be required to complete a total of seven units.

The core units that you must successfully complete are

- organizational performance and culture in practice,
- evidence-based practice, and
- professional behaviours and valuing people.

The specialist units that must also be successfully completed are

- supporting self-directed and social learning,
- learning and development design to create value, and
- facilitating personalized and performance-focused learning.

It is then possible to select one additional specialist unit to make up the total required credits for this qualification (again, forty-two credits). Learners are required to choose from the following list:

- specialist employment law;
- advances in digital learning and development;
- learning and development essentials;
- people management in an international context;
- diversity and inclusion;
- leadership and management development;
- well-being at work.

Advanced Diploma in Strategic People Management

To be awarded a level 7 Advanced Diploma in Strategic People Management you will be required to complete a total of eight units.

The core units that you must successfully complete are

- work and working lives in a changing business environment,
- people management and development strategies for performance,

- personal effectiveness, ethics and business acumen, and
- business research in people practice.

The specialist units that you must successfully complete are

- strategic employment relations,
- resourcing and talent management to sustain success and
- strategic reward management.

It is then possible to select one additional specialist unit to make up the total required credits for this qualification (120 credits). Learners are required to choose from the following list:

- organizational design and development;
- advanced employment law in practice;
- learning and development practice;
- technology enhanced learning;
- advanced diversity and inclusion;
- managing people in an international context;
- well-being at work.

Advanced Diploma in Strategic Learning and Development

To be awarded a level 7 advanced diploma in strategic learning and development you will be required to complete a total of eight units.

The four core units that you must successfully complete are

- work and working lives in a changing business environment,
- people management and development strategies for performance,
- personal effectiveness, ethics and business acumen, and
- business research in people practice.

The three specialist units that must also be successfully completed are

- organization design and development,
- leadership and management development in context, and
- designing learning to improve performance.

In addition to the seven units above, it is then possible to select one additional specialist unit to make up the total required credits for this qualification (120 credits). Learners are required to choose from the following list:

- advanced employment law in practice;
- learning and development practice;
- technology-enhanced learning;
- advanced diversity and inclusion;
- managing people in an international context;
- well-being at work.

Assessment

CIPD assessments have been designed in accordance with the evolving nature of the profession. Assessments take many forms but there are no exams in the new qualification structure at any level. Assessment documents include slide decks and presenter notes, guidance leaflets, case studies, analyses of data, briefing documents, reflective journals, interview preparation, simulated interviews with peers, narratives, fact sheets, formal business reports, continuing professional development (CPD) portfolios, assessment questions and business research projects. These provide a good range of work-aligned assessments from which to develop core skills, knowledge and competencies.

Mode of delivery

Studying for CIPD qualifications has become increasingly flexible, and they now allow you to effectively balance learning with your work and personal life. If you are thinking about studying, you might consider how much time you would like to dedicate to your studies each week and whether you are able to attend a class or if you prefer to learn online, either via distance learning or through live online sessions.

You can choose to study through a university or a private training provider. Having taught at both, I have found that universities are most likely to have entry points in September and January. The larger private providers offer what are sometimes called 'roll-on roll-off' programmes. which allow you to start at any point in the year. I have taught students that have literally signed up the previous day! These private providers are also more flexible about the speed at which you can progress through the programme due to their flexible modes of delivery. If you are taking a few months off from work, it enables you to fast-track your qualification, while for those who are juggling their working and personal lives, a slower pace of study to suit personal circumstances is possible.

On the other hand, universities offer much more in the way of support, including library resources and access to a number of research databases so that learners are able to use a wide range of e-journals, e-books and magazine subscriptions for wider reading and research. Universities also have student support departments that provide everything from advice about student finance, including which bursaries and hardship funds are available, to information on finding accommodation. In addition, they offer mental health support, such as counselling and emotional-support networks, study-buddy programmes, a wide range of careers support, and specialist academic support in areas such as referencing, maths and statistics, as well as academic writing.

Getting qualified with the SHRI

The SHRI Academy is a training institution that supports both local and international adult learners through a range of academic programmes, from basic certificates to master's degrees. It works with UK university partners to deliver top-up qualifications in HR management. It delivers a range of certificates in payroll administration and HR management, as well as diplomas in HR leadership with business partnering, organizational psychology and compensation and benefits management.

Certification can be achieved through the Institute for Human Resource Professionals (IHRP). It is necessary to demonstrate competence in the following categories.

Mindsets and behaviours

- Display business and financial acumen
- Demonstrate change leadership
- Adopt a future orientation
- Uphold professional conduct

Functional competencies

- Plan: resource planning, financial budgeting, long-term strategic workforce planning and change
- Attract: sourcing, selecting, securing and onboarding of talent
- Develop: learning and development, career development, performance management, talent management, succession planning
- Engage: workforce motivation including compensation and benefits, people engagement, cross-cultural management
- Separate: voluntary and involuntary exits and retirement

Foundational competencies

- Analytics and insights
- Relationships and communication

- Technology and operational excellence
- Labour policies and legislation

IHRP certification includes both the experience and development pathways. There are four different levels of progression: IHRP certified associate (IHRP-CA), IHRP certified professional (IHRP-CP), IHRP senior professional (IHRP-SP) and IHRP master professional (IHRP-MP).

The IHRP-CA level is available through the development pathway and is designed for new and aspiring HR professionals working towards the certified professional qualification. The pathway is designed for those who do not meet the eligibility criteria of the experience pathway. The programme is available to working professionals, junior HR specialists and HR administrators who do not possess an HR-related degree. The qualification is also designed for recent graduates, focusing on the application of HR knowledge.

The IHRP-CA route includes three stages of development. In stage 1, the pre-qualification stage, learners take paper A, which focuses on employment policy and legislation, and paper N, which concentrates on foundational HR knowledge and competencies, as detailed in the competency framework discussed above. Stage 2 is designed along the '3Es framework', which includes 'emerging' skills (through projects, micro-credentials, frameworks, workshops and tools); 'exposure' to mentoring, networking and learning; and 'education' through communities of practice, mobile-learning platforms and courses in emerging HR skills provided by accredited partners. Stage 3 is the progression route to paper B in the IHRP-CP level, which includes functional and foundation competencies and an experience assessment on HR experience and education.

To gain IHRP-CP status learners will be required to successfully complete papers A and B, and for IHRP-SP status learners will need to complete papers A and C. For IHRP-MP status assessment will take the form of a structured professional dialogue.

The IHRP-CP level is for those with 2 years or more of HR experience who are responsible for developing and implementing HR policies and programmes to deliver HR services. Assessment is through the online submission of detailed information and documented proof to demonstrate HR-related training and experience. Candidates are also required to complete a computer-based assessment comprising multiple-choice questions for papers A and B.

The IHRP-SP level is for experienced HR leaders who are responsible for leading an HR function and designing and developing HR policies and programmes. Assessment is through the online submission of detailed information and documented proof to demonstrate HR-related training and experience. Candidates are also required to complete a computer-based assessment comprising multiple-choice questions for paper A and short-answer questions for paper C.

The IHRP-MP level is conducted via an open application process and a professional discussion process once a year.

Assessment

Paper A covers labour policies and legislation. This is a 90-minute open-book examination. It consists of thirty multiple-choice and situational-judgement questions.

Paper B covers functional and foundational competencies with a focus on mindsets and behaviours. This is a 2-hour closed-book examination. It includes six scenarios and a total of thirty multiple-choice questions.

Paper C covers functional and foundational competencies with a focus on mindsets and behaviours. This is a 3-hour closed-book examination. It covers three scenarios and a total of twelve short-answer questions.

Getting qualified with the IHRMP

The IHRMP is the professional body that seeks to advance HR practice in Ghana. Its professional certification programme provides not only a qualification for practising HR professionals but also training for polytechnic and university graduates who would like to practise HR in organizations. Launched in 2002, the minimum entry requirement for the four-level programme is a higher national diploma (HND) or a first degree in any discipline. Successful completion of the four levels leads to certified HR practitioner status.

A prospective student with any degree or HND will start from level 1. Those with a degree or master's degree in HR will start from level 3. There is the possibility to gain subject exemptions at levels 1 and 2 for those who have successfully completed courses that align with the syllabus.

The programme is structured into four levels, as follows.

- Level 1 includes papers on the principles of management, an introduction to HRM, general psychology and business statistics.
- Level 2 includes papers on organizational behaviour, an introduction to HR development, the fundamentals of accounting and an introduction to industrial relations.
- Level 3 includes papers on legal aspects of HRM, industrial relations practice, recruitment and compensation management, HR development practice and business communication.
- Level 4 includes the candidate's presentation of project work and 3 years' work experience in HR.

Members who have successfully completed the professional certification programme and remain in good standing are listed on the institute's website, and this is updated annually.

Getting qualified with the AHRI

The AHRI introduced HR certification to set the bar for HR practice in Australia. Their HR qualifications define what good HR is and they prepare practitioners for business partner roles in their respective organizations.

HR certification can be achieved by taking one of four different pathways.

- Pathway 1 – the AHRI Practising Certification Program – is designed for mid-level to senior-level HR practitioners/consultants.
- Pathway 2 – the Senior Leaders Pathway – is designed for senior-level to executive-level HR practitioners/consultants.
- Pathway 3 – the CIPD Reciprocity or IHRP Mutual Recognition Pathway – is designed for chartered members/IHRP-certified professionals from the UK and Singapore institutes, respectively.
- Pathway 4 – the Academic Pathway – is designed for HR academics.

Aspiring HR professionals

For those seeking a career in HR there are a number of entry points, including student membership, graduate membership and affiliate membership.

For those with less than 5 years of experience in HR, the AHRI offers a number of CPD opportunities, including short courses and webinars, as well as the AHRI nationally accredited Certificate IV in Human Resources, which is designed for aspiring HR professionals and provides an introduction to HR and business strategy, talent and organizational goals, workplace legislation, and health and safety.

AHRI Practising Certification Program

For those with at least 5 years of HR experience, or HR graduates with at least 2 years HR experience, the AHRI Practising Certification Program provides a solid underpinning to achieve certified HR practitioner status.

This programme requires completion of the following four units of study.

- Unit 1: information on the strategic HR professional.
- Unit 2: information on the HR organizational environment.
- Unit 3: information on workforce design, development and performance.
- Unit 4: an applied project in organizational capability.

Applicants must hold current AHRI professional membership as part of the entry requirements for this programme. Assessment is via a range of tasks across the units, including written response tasks, practical work-based reports, learning journals and critical analysis essays.

Senior Leaders Pathway

The Senior Leaders Pathway recognizes the wealth of experience that professionals have collected over the years, acknowledging HR skills, knowledge and behaviours acquired in implementing organizational change.

To achieve certification senior leaders must submit a case study of an HR initiative that they have implemented in the last 5 years, and they must demonstrate how it has impacted their business (a case study from 5–8 years ago might be considered). This is followed by an interview with the National Certification Council, which reviews the application.

The pathway is designed for those with more than 10 years' experience in generalist HR, including 5 years' experience in senior leadership/management. Experience should include budgetary and strategic responsibilities, the responsibility of leading a team to achieve organizational goals, and completion of AHRI-accredited or relevant postgraduate qualifications or equivalent knowledge, skills and experience. AHRI members can also apply for a fellowship position at the time of their application.

CIPD Reciprocity Pathway

The CIPD Reciprocity Pathway is available to those who have already achieved the equivalent of certified practitioner or academic status by attaining the chartered/academic member or fellow positions with the CIPD in the UK.

IHRP Mutual Recognition Pathway

This pathway is available to HR practitioners who have achieved the IHRP certified professional, IHRP senior professional or IHRP master professional levels with the Singapore Human Resources Institute.

Academic Pathway

The Academic Pathway offers experienced and senior academics an opportunity to become a certified academic HR member in recognition of their professional contribution to HR thinking and knowledge through academic research and/or teaching. HR academic certification can be awarded at the Certified Academic HR level or the Fellow Certified Academic HR level depending on experience and academic contribution. Academic member HR status is a non-certified membership that is available to those who do not meet the requirements set out above.

Reciprocal qualification arrangements

The CIPD is working to increase its global reach and is increasingly partnering with awarding bodies to provide reciprocal recognition of people management experience and qualifications.

An individual with a CIPD qualification who wishes to work in Europe is required to apply for recognition/comparability within the country concerned. It is important to understand individual employer requirements. The CIPD is comparable to other institutions in the European qualifications framework, which is a common European reference framework that links countries' qualification systems together.

BEING A GLOBAL HR PROFESSIONAL

In this chapter I have discussed the professional qualification routes for five different awarding bodies. The selected professional bodies provide an insight into the differences and similarities when gaining accreditation across different continents, and, more importantly, they highlight the global reach of qualifications and the possibilities for recognition in different country contexts, in support of a global career. Although employment law differs from country to country, good people management practices are at the core of the profession worldwide, presenting many opportunities to develop an international career in people management.

Businesses are increasingly international and it may be that you will have the opportunity to build international experience early on in your career. Being flexible and adaptable, understanding commonalities and differences across cultures, resourcing talent internationally, and developing positive working relationships are essential skills to develop a successful career in people management. Undertaking accredited qualifications can support you in developing the essential underpinning theory through research, tools and models to support your international development.

SUMMARY

Although it is not essential, getting certified with a professional body can provide you with a competitive advantage in the job market. It is particularly helpful if you are commencing a career in people management as it can provide the core knowledge required to be an effective practitioner and can help you accelerate your career. The actual process to certification varies across professional bodies but most institutes follow a developmental path that recognizes previous qualifications and experience. In some cases there is also the possibility of achieving certification through an experience assessment for those with demonstrable experience. It is therefore possible to get certified at any point in your career, whether you possess little or a great deal of experience, for both entry-level careers and promotions.

Chapter 5

HR FOR SCHOOL LEAVERS AND GRADUATES

IT IS POSSIBLE TO GET started in people management at any age as the profession offers multiple entry points. This chapter discusses the opportunities for both school leavers and graduates. It explores the apprenticeship route to career entry in the UK as an alternative to a degree. It also looks at whether one's choice of degree subject matters for entry into the profession. Various degree subjects are explored in relation to preparing for a career in HR, along with professional body accreditations that may or may not be included in a degree. Case study examples are included from a range of people professionals who share their experiences of getting started in HR, including their route into the profession. Finally, we discuss how to gain valuable work experience in order to enhance your application.

UK APPRENTICESHIP ROUTES INTO THE PEOPLE PROFESSION

Apprenticeships are paid roles that essentially provide training on the job in combination with off-the-job learning. In the UK, apprenticeships are offered in both HR and learning and development. Apprenticeships last for a minimum of 12 months but must be completed in 20 months, and the training can be delivered by a registered college, university or independent training provider that delivers the formal development in partnership with the employer and the work-based training. The CIPD is approved to carry out the assessment activities that take place at the end of the apprenticeship training programme.

Level 3 apprenticeships

There are two apprenticeships available at level 3: the HR support apprenticeship and the learning and development practitioner apprenticeship. Both provide entry routes to their respective pathways.

Level 3 HR support apprenticeship

In this role you will likely be handling day-to-day queries and you will provide some advice and key HR information to the business in line with company policy and current legislation. You will use the HR systems in the organization to keep records and you will gain experience throughout the employee lifecycle, from recruitment to exit. You will liaise with a range of stakeholders across the organization, from employees to line managers.

Entry requirements

The level 3 apprenticeship is equivalent to an A level standard of education (advanced level qualifications that are taken at age 18 in the UK). Initial assessment explores what the apprentice has already achieved (prior learning) and what they are capable of achieving (potential). Applicants must hold level 2 qualifications in English and mathematics (a GCSE or equivalent in the UK, i.e. the school leaving certificate at age 16) and these must be completed prior to taking the end-point assessment.

Assessment

The end-point assessment consists of a project in which the candidate takes a consultative role and then undertakes a professional discussion; both are assessed against the knowledge, skills and behaviours required for level 3.

Apprenticeship certification and CIPD membership

Associate membership will be offered to all apprentices who successfully complete end-point assessment with the CIPD.

Level 3 learning and development practitioner apprenticeship

The learning and development practitioner may work across the private, public or third sectors, helping to improve performance in the workplace at the individual, team and organizational levels. Working with HR colleagues and specialist learning and development colleagues, the learning and development practitioner will work with subject-matter experts across the business in support of all aspects of the learning cycle, from the identification of learning needs to the design, delivery and evaluation of learning interventions. The apprenticeship development programme typically takes 18–24 months to complete.

Entry requirements

Level 2 English and mathematics are required prior to taking the end-point assessment.

Assessment

Modes of assessment test occupational competence against the skills, knowledge and behaviours required for learning outcomes. This includes a work-based project, taking the form of a business report on a learning solution designed in response to a real business problem, followed by a 60-minute competency-based interview. The assessment is supported by a learning-journal 20-minute presentation with a 25-minute question-and-answer session.

Apprenticeship certification and CIPD membership

Associate membership will be offered to all apprentices who successfully complete end-point assessment with the CIPD.

Level 5 apprenticeships

Two level 5 apprenticeships are offered: the HR consultant/partner apprenticeship and the learning and development consultant/business partner apprenticeship.

Level 5 HR consultant/partner apprenticeship

This apprenticeship is aimed at HR professionals who are leading on people initiatives, making decisions and recommendations on people plans, influencing managers about good practice, leading on people projects, and aligning work with organizational priorities. The qualification is comparable to a diploma in higher education and typically take 12 months to complete (and no longer than 32 months).

Entry requirements

Applicants should be 18 or over and need to live in England. They will typically have two or more A levels.

Assessment

The assessment process takes the form of a project in which the candidate takes a consultative role and also a professional discussion; both are assessed against the knowledge, skills and behaviours required for level 5. Assessment is carried out by CIPD assessors who have strong backgrounds in HR and who have been assessing against the HR standards for at least 5 years.

Level 5 learning and development consultant/business partner apprenticeship

This apprenticeship typically takes 18–24 months. The apprentice will work alongside colleagues who specialize in HR and report to a senior learning and development manager, head of department or director.

Entry requirements

Apprentices without level 2 qualifications in English and mathematics will need to achieve these prior to taking the end-point assessment. Applicants will typically have two or more A levels.

Assessment

Assessment includes a work-based project with a professional discussion and a learning-journal presentation. The work-based project is a formal report that requires the apprentice to demonstrate learning and development consultancy skills, and it is followed by a 75-minute competency-based interview. The learning-journal presentation is based on the learning journal and is a 15-minute presentation with a 30-minute question and answer session.

Level 7 apprenticeships

The level 7 apprenticeship has been designed for senior HR professionals, senior learning and development professionals and senior organization development professionals.

Level 7 senior people professional apprenticeship

Designed by the L&D/HR Trailblazer Group and approved by the Institute for Apprenticeships and Technical Education, the senior people professional apprenticeship was launched in 2021 and is designed for those working at an operational level who wish to move into a more strategic role. This apprenticeship might suit those who have completed a level 5 apprenticeship in HR or learning and development and are now ready to progress in their career, or those working in management but not necessarily in HR/learning and development. It might also be incorporated into a fast-track graduate programme. Successful completion of this programme prepares professionals for CIPD chartered membership. The programme takes 24–36 months to complete depending on existing knowledge, skills and experience.

Assessment

The programme is assessed through a professional discussion, which is underpinned by a portfolio of evidence. This is supported by a project proposal presentation and a question-and-answer session.

Case studies

Now let us explore some case studies of people professionals who have gained their qualifications and experience through the apprenticeship route.

Jenny

I loved school but hated exams. I was quite good at coursework and I was happy if I could just work at my own pace to get things done. I have a hopeless memory and just couldn't remember enough for exams. I did stay on and do A levels in business studies, ICT and English but I just couldn't face another 3 years of study for a degree. I was lucky to gain some work experience in HR for a few weeks and this gave me the bug for all things 'people'.

I saw a vacancy for an HR apprenticeship at a design and property consultancy and I was successful. They liked my outgoing personality and confidence and they thought I would fit in well. They liked the fact that I knew what HR was all about as I had already had some experience in a different organization.

The apprenticeship lasted for about 18 months and then I was promoted, first to people assistant and now people officer. I completed the level 3 CIPD qualification during my apprenticeship and right now I'm just about to start my CIPD level 7.

Gill

I did actually plan to go to university and I did complete year 1 of a degree in business. The problem was I found it just wasn't for me. I was working part time paying for my studies and I just thought I would be better off getting some work experience and earning some money. I saw an apprenticeship role in HR advertised at my local airport and thought it sounded really exciting. I was successful and that was the start of my career as a people professional. I completed my apprenticeship in just over 15 months and I was then promoted to resourcing assistant, then to resourcing coordinator and now resourcing partner. I'm really keen to progress my career in HR.

Callum

I was keen to develop my career in the workplace and so I opted for an apprenticeship position rather than take a degree. I learn best on the job and I enjoy shadowing my colleagues, getting involved with different projects [and] attending meetings. It has been really fantastic to be immersed in the business, to learn the jargon [and] how to be a people professional. I'm hoping to stay on with my organization after I complete my apprenticeship.

While the apprenticeship route is becoming increasingly popular as an entry into people management, the graduate route is still more common. We will therefore discuss that next.

THE GRADUATE ROUTE

Over the years I have worked with many graduate learners from all disciplines: English, history, geography, philosophy, classics and many more. The most popular choices include psychology, law and, of course, human resource management. Sometimes learners have a career direction in mind – accountancy, say, or law – only to find, a year or two into their chosen role, that this was not the right choice for them. Business and psychology graduates might benefit from their previous studies when taking people management qualifications, but overall it is transferable skills that can really help. Being able to critically analyse and evaluate in order to find new insights takes time and training. Degrees that prepare learners in these skills provide a great platform for both further study and professional practice.

If you are certain that you want to follow a career in people management, you may decide to undertake a degree in this area. Some universities provide professional accreditation in addition to awarding degrees. This means that they have mapped their programmes onto the structure of an awarding body such as the CIPD. Opting for a degree that is accredited by the professional body of your choice will save you time and money in the long term. If you are searching for a degree in people management, do consider whether the programme includes professional body accreditation – not all of them do!

In some countries undergraduate programmes include underpinning knowledge that will support you in your preparation for professional assessment. If you are certain that you would like to pursue a career in people management, it may be a good idea to explore the professional-assessment requirements before you commence your degree to ensure that the content will effectively prepare you for professional membership.

Let us take a look at some case studies to learn more about graduate choices and entry into the profession.

Freddie

I have a bachelor's degree in psychology and this is where I first started learning about organizational psychology and design. This led me to start my career as a recruiter and then after that I found opportunities to broaden my horizons and to become a people management generalist.

Catherina

I studied law with a view to becoming a barrister in the UK. I found it really competitive and I struggled to find a pupillage (work-based experience). I found a temporary role as a people administrator and found that I really enjoyed the variety and working in an organization. I'm now going to study for my professional qualifications.

Rhianna

I studied business because I wasn't too sure of what I actually wanted to do. I then found a role as an intern in a large recruitment organization. This was great, I really enjoyed it and knew then that I wanted to pursue a career in people management. I found a job as an HR Assistant for a large food company and I stayed there for 2 years. This gave me great foundation experience and I then moved to the motor industry as an HR generalist. I've been with my current employer for 5 years now and I've been promoted to HR Business Partner.

Tobi

I have a bachelor's degree in psychology, followed by a master's degree in business administration and HR management. I started my career as a recruiter in a recruitment agency and then after 1 year I moved to an engineering company where I spent 4 years working as an HR generalist. I now work as an HR manager in a healthcare company.

Rubella

I read for a degree in history and then I took a master's in labour and psychology. I also have a master's degree in management. My first role was as an HR generalist in a beer production company. I then worked in water production and now communications. I did work for some years as a consultant.

Sinbad

I was always interested in languages so I studied French and Spanish as an undergraduate degree and then I decided that I wanted to become an accountant. I found an entry-level role and gained my professional qualifications. The problem was I hated it. I wanted to work with people as I'm quite social. I had a career break with my first child and studied for a people management qualification. I've now found my first people position with a training organization.

Sarah

I graduated with a maths degree thinking that I was going to become an actuary. I gained a graduate training place but ended up failing my professional exams. I just didn't enjoy the role and thought that the people team seemed to be having more fun. I gained an entry level role as HR Assistant and then progressed in that organization.

Jane

I studied geography as an undergraduate only to find that there were not that many opportunities to use my degree after graduation. I started as an HR administrator in a further education college and then I worked my way up the career ladder to my current position, which is senior talent partner in a university.

WORK EXPERIENCE

No matter what your starting point, getting some insight into what a people practitioner actually does is a great asset for your CV. Any work experience you can get in the profession is helpful; maybe you have family or friends who can help you secure a week or two of shadowing others on the job? If not, do liaise with teachers, lecturers, careers advisors, work experience placement coordinators – anyone and everyone who might be able to help. Do not be afraid to ask for help. People need to know what you would like to do and what you are seeking and you will be surprised at the possibilities that might appear. There are a number of ways you might add to this early experience and we will explore these below.

INTERNSHIPS

An internship is a period of work offered by an employer to a student or a graduate in order to provide specific industry experience that may relate to the field of study being undertaken. Typically, internships last anything from a week to a year, and they can be paid or voluntary. This on-the-job experience can provide real insights into your chosen profession while also helping you to develop important soft skills such as time management, communication, interpersonal skills, team working, decision making, self-motivation and leadership.

Internship opportunities are advertised through job sites. At the time of writing I found the following three examples.

Jeffries Group LLC human resources internship – London[17]

Jeffries Group LLC is the largest independent, global, full-time investment banking firm, head quartered in the United States. The company specializes in providing insight, expertise and execution to investors, companies and governments. It provides a full range of investment banking, advisory, sales and trading, research and wealth management services across all products in the Americas, Europe and Asia.

Jeffries summer internships provide an opportunity to gain insights into a global, client-focused investment bank and to experience an entrepreneurial environment where employees are able to make an immediate impact and are rewarded for performance. The 10-week training programme includes an orientation, social and educational events, an opportunity to develop and grow your network and real responsibility for day-to-day tasks with the support of a mentor.

Key responsibilities

- *Supporting HR and recruitment projects from a project/event coordination, communication and implementation perspective*
- *Providing support for various HR initiatives you are assigned to, and being willing to help where required across the team*

Requirements

- *Penultimate-year undergraduate*
- *Proficient in Microsoft Office: Outlook, Word, Excel and PowerPoint*
- *Strong verbal and written communication skills*
- *Team player*

- *Excellent interpersonal skills, ability to communicate at all levels*
- *Positive attitude and the desire to learn and grow*
- *Professionalism, assertiveness and confidentiality*

Amazon human resources internship – virtual location[18]

Amazon is a company of builders. A philosophy of ownership carries through everything we do – from the proprietary technologies we create to the new businesses we launch and grow. You'll find it in every team across our company; from providing Earth's biggest selection of products to developing ground-breaking software and devices that change entire industries, Amazon embraces invention and progressive thinking. Amazon is continually evolving; it's a place where motivated employees thrive, and ownership and accountability lead to meaningful results. It's as simple as this: we pioneer.

With every order made and parcel delivered, customer demand at Amazon is growing. And to meet this demand, and keep our world-class service running smoothly, we're growing our operations team across Europe. Delivering hundreds of thousands of products to hundreds of countries, our operations teams rely on support from a variety of human resources teams to meet the growing needs of Amazonians across Europe.

The opportunity

Whatever your background, if you love learning what it takes to hire and develop the best, enjoy building plans to attract, retain, develop and support growing teams, effectively communicating across diverse teams in multiple countries, Amazon is a great place to be. Because it's only by coming up with new ideas and challenging the status quo that we can continue to be the most customer-centric company on Earth. We're all about flexibility: we expect you to adapt to changes quickly and we encourage you to try new things. Amazon is looking for ambitious and enthusiastic students to join our fast-paced world as interns. An Amazon EU internship will provide you with an unforgettable experience in a fast-paced, dynamic and international environment; it will boost your resumé and will provide a superb introduction to our activities.

General Electric HR people science internship – London[19]

Want to be a pioneer in a fast-growing area of HR? Have a mathematical or statistical background and interested in HR? HR functions are on the edge of shifting to data-driven decisions, utilizing data on their most important asset – people. The GE renewable energy HR team are looking for a graduate intern with a data science background to join the strategic workforce planning and HR operations team to help implement more data-driven decision making within HR.

GE ... drives the world forward by tackling its biggest challenges. By combining world-class engineering with software and analytics, GE helps the world work more efficiently, reliably and safely. GE people are global, diverse and dedicated, operating with the highest integrity and passion to fulfil GE's mission and deliver for our customers.

The opportunity

This is a 12-month internship focusing on embedding data science into the HR processes within the GE renewable energy HR team.

Key responsibilities

- *Supporting the HR leadership team with people-related data-driven insights taken from statistical analyses of HR data sets*
- *Summarizing and providing graphical visualizations on key people metrics such as diversity, attrition, promotions and more*
- *Leading on development of key algorithms around attrition, diversity, culture and other important people metrics*

- *Partnering with HR leaders on designing data research, defining hypotheses, data collection and running multiple different statistical models*
- *Effectively using HR reporting tools and dashboards to provide ad hoc support to the HR leadership team*
- *Assisting in development on future-of-work steering committee and educational material for the HR team*
- *Assisting in monitoring of data quality and holding HRMs accountable with their data ownership*

Requirements

- *Bachelor's, Master's degree or PhD in data science, mathematics, statistics, computer science, economics or related scientific field of study*
- *Coursework in statistics and application of statistical tools*
- *Working knowledge of Tableau*
- *Fluency in English, with polite, professional communication skills*
- *Intermediate to advanced knowledge of applied statistical techniques and statistical packages, i.e. R, Python, SPSS or other*
- *The ability to prioritize multiple tasks and work to deadlines*
- *Previous experience in a customer operations or an HR role within a multinational organization*
- *Experience in MS Office Suite with expert skills in MS Excel, Access and PowerPoint*
- *Strongly developed analytical skills with the ability to assess data and trends using both quantitative and qualitative analysis techniques, including being able to execute data extraction, data mining and reporting from a variety of workforce systems*
- *A keen interest in HR along with excellent written, verbal and problem-solving skills*
- *The ability to communicate with employees at all levels*

Internships vary in length, from a few weeks to perhaps a year. They are usually aimed at students, particularly undergraduates, and they can be part time during semesters or full time in the holiday period. Internships are a great way to enhance your CV and demonstrate a real commitment to your chosen profession. However, they are not the only way to gain valuable experience. You may decide to opt for a degree that includes a placement and/or a year abroad, and this is discussed next.

INDUSTRY PLACEMENTS/A YEAR ABROAD

When you are researching undergraduate programmes, you may opt for a degree that provides a work-placement year. This is usually optional but it does provide a very useful opportunity to gain practical experience. Universities provide students with support in finding placements through the connections they have built with employers through regular events and presentations. The placement provides the opportunity to develop your professional skills and to make connections between academic learning and the workplace. It allows you to consider how the theories you have studied can be used in practice and how management practices might be improved.

When you undertake a placement year you are usually employed by the company and you will undertake a role very similar to a graduate-level position. The placement provides the opportunity to develop transferable skills that will improve your performance in your future career. Specifically, you will be able to develop skills like team working, presentations, project management, negotiation and organizational skills. You can find out what you enjoy and learn more about the profession while also increasing your chances of successful employment after university.

In the UK a placement year usually occurs between the penultimate year of your degree and the final one. You then return to university for your final year. European universities often offer a semester abroad. You will remain a student of your university during the placement and you are likely to have an assignment to complete that is related to your experience. It is likely that a dedicated tutor will be allocated to you to ensure that you are supported during the period, and together you will complete regular progress reports. The placement year is usually paid and the salary will depend on the sector that you choose to work in.

During my career in the HR industry I have supported numerous undergraduates with placements. Here is one of their stories.

Case study

Carlos was a management student from the University of Toulouse in France. He was keen to gain workplace experience in the UK and to improve his English. He worked alongside my colleagues and me in an organization in central London. During his 3-month placement Carlos gained experience in each of the company's functions: marketing, sales, operations, learning and development, commercial, people and culture. He attended all meetings with both internal and external stakeholders, worked on a project to analyse learner feedback, made recommendations to improve the delivery of programmes, undertook research relating to the implementation of a new HR system, supported all aspects of administration, and assisted with the organization of events.

'I really enjoyed my placement and I gained some valuable work experience. It was great to be able to live in London and experience a different culture. As I spoke and wrote in English every day my language skills improved.'

VOLUNTEERING

It may be that a placement year or an internship is not quite right for you and that you are seeking to gain experience in a more flexible form. If so, volunteering might be an option. These positions are not paid but they do provide the opportunity to gain valuable work experience while learning from others. Opportunities are varied and might include general administration, data analysis, events organizing, recruitment and many more areas.

At the time of writing I found the following voluntary roles.

Teenage Helpline HR administrator voluntary role – UK[20]

[We are] an online mentoring service run by young people to be used by young people. The aims of Teenage Helpline are to provide the first stepping stone for young people who may need to get professional support, but do not feel comfortable seeking this support for themselves. Mentoring is also available for young people who do not need professional support but who need additional help ... with other personal issues.

The opportunity

This role is an opportunity for an enthusiastic and proactive individual to join the people team at Teenage Helpline. The role would suit someone who is looking to enter the world of HR. You'll be the first point of contact for all our new volunteers and you'll make job offers and onboard new volunteers into the Teenage Helpline family. You'll also provide a helpdesk service for existing volunteers and their HR-related queries.'

Requirements

- *Excellent communication and customer service skills*
- *Good skills in IT and proficient use of Microsoft applications*

- *Ability to manage and prioritize own workload*
- *Ability to work effectively and independently within a team*
- *Attention to detail*

This is a remote-working role and candidates will be required to have access to a computer, the internet and a comfortable space to work at home. Working hours are flexible and candidates will be required to work approximately 2 hours per week.

Travellers Aid HR volunteer coordinator – Australia[21]

Travellers Aid's goal is to be the recognized expert in the delivery of services to people facing travel-related challenges. [Our] vision is a society where people with mobility challenges are treated with dignity and respect, being able to lead full and rich lives with confidence. [Our] mission is to empower people with travel-related challenges to connect, engage and participate within their local communities through the use of public transport. Travellers Aid's workforce consists of 75% dedicated volunteers and 25% staff.

The opportunity

The Travellers Aid volunteering programme (6–12 months) offers an opportunity to get involved in the disability services and community sector, gain a range of valuable experiences and connect with other enthusiastic volunteers. The programme offers a range of opportunities assisting service users with permanent disability, temporary impairment or those with age-related mobility challenges. The volunteer will coordinate, recruit, onboard, train, develop and provide support to the volunteers and site supervisors. They will create a valuable experience for volunteers at Travellers Aid and initiate new opportunities to expand the volunteering positions available.'

Requirements

- *Qualification/experience in business administration, human resources or similar field*
- *Competency in cloud-based IT systems including Microsoft Office applications*
- *A basic understanding of HR principles, frameworks and change management*
- *A commitment to value-based workforce management*

Dallas Pets Alive recruitment coordinator – US[22]

Dallas Pets Alive's mission is to promote and provide the resources, education and programmes needed to eliminate the killing of companion animals in North Texas. The rescue programme focuses on rescuing healthy and treatable pets at North Texas shelters at the greatest risk of being euthanized, reducing owner surrender through the positive alternatives to the shelter surrender programme, opening up kennel space by transporting pets to partners in the US and Canada in need of adoptable animals and challenging the way that the community views rescue animals.

The opportunity

Reporting to the assistant director of recruitment, this role will interact with members of the volunteer team. Responsibilities will include driving the orientation for new volunteers through managing sign-ups using Eventbrite (sending reminder emails, tracking attendance, sending follow-up emails), coordinating guest speakers, managing content (updating slide decks, creating guest speaker slides) and participating in a rotating schedule to include presenting and being on call for technical support. The volunteer will also be encouraged to suggest new ideas to engage volunteers and continuously improve the sessions.

Requirements

- *Higher degree of education*
- *Interest and/or experience in human resources and talent acquisition/recruiting a plus*
- *Proficiency with use of Gmail and Google applications (Google Sheets, Slides, Docs and Meet)*
- *Experience with Zoom a plus, but not required*
- *Ability to work within deadlines and manage multiple priorities*
- *Curiosity to learn and a willingness to think outside the box and go against the status quo*
- *Must not have conflicting associations with similar non-profit organizations or business(es) related to animal welfare*

This is a remote-working role with plenty of opportunities to get involved in other projects depending on the time the volunteer has available.

SUMMARY

We have explored the various routes for entry into the people profession, with a particular focus on apprenticeships and graduate opportunities. We have discussed the importance of gaining work experience and how this might be achieved. By including internship and voluntary vacancies from an international/multinational perspective I have attempted to highlight the openings available in different country contexts. Similar prospects are likely to be available in your region and I would encourage you to explore these opportunities as soon as you are able to. Apprenticeships provide an opportunity to gain work experience and professional accreditations simultaneously. Degrees provide a sound base from which to launch a career in the people profession but education alone is unlikely to secure a graduate entry position. Gaining work experience in one way or another will help you to stand out from the competition.

Chapter 6

HR FOR CAREER CHANGERS

IT IS NEVER TOO LATE to transition to a new role, and having some previous work experience can work to your advantage in the people profession. A great way to prepare for career change is to explore job profiles and their entry requirements. This will provide you with a platform from which to assess where you are and where you wish to go. This chapter provides insights into transferable skills and, using case study examples, reveals how others have made the transition. Various roles are considered across the public, private and third sectors to help you identify the kinds of opportunity that await you and to help you decide the right level at which to pitch your applications for entry into the profession.

GETTING STARTED

Before diving in and assessing potential roles that might suit your skills and experience, it might be worthwhile to take a step back and assess your current position. What really interests you? What gets you out of bed in the morning? What do you value?

Consider the following questions.

- Do you enjoy telling others what they need to do?
- Do you find it easy to make decisions quickly?
- Do you enjoy taking responsibility for others?

- Are you comfortable with influencing others?
- Do you enjoy talking in front of a group of people?
- Do you like meeting new people?
- Do you enjoy making things better for others?
- Do you like solving complicated things?
- Do you like working with facts?

Also ask yourself whether you prefer to work

- alone or in a group;
- in an office or remotely;
- in a full-time, part-time or flexible role;
- in a small, medium or large organization;
- in the public, private or third sector?

Activity
You might like to make some notes about your interests, motivations, preferences and values in the table below so that you can align your job search with your identified requirements.

TRANSFERABLE SKILLS

When we are looking to change career, it is likely we have developed multiple skills and significant knowledge that will support us in our new role. Transferable skills are those core skills and abilities that can be applied to a wide range of different jobs and industries. You are likely to have developed these skills through previous work experience, whether paid or voluntary, and through hobbies or your work in managing the home. Transferable skills might include areas such as leadership, time management, communication, delegation, problem-solving, data analysis, adaptability, project management or technical literacy, to name just a few. The important ability here is to identify your transferable skills and knowledge and then to effectively articulate this to future employers. It is not just a case of listing our transferable skills but rather a case of reflecting on examples that can support an application (see the examples that follow).

Communication

Rather than stating that you have good communication skills, you might say:

> As a sales coordinator for a national furniture chain I presented a summary of sales lead responses to the senior management team every Monday. This meeting was instrumental in the sales team plan for the week, helping to identify priorities and supporting the allocation of regional work.

Problem-solving

You may be a great problem-solver but you need to provide evidence of how you have used your skills. Here is an example of what you might say:

> As an accountant for a small engineering company I was required to work with stakeholders to implement the new business software. As the finance expert I analysed requirements, tested the system and became the 'go-to' person for technological problems.

Time management

Instead of confirming that you have well-developed time-management skills, you might explain:

> As a senior content editor for life sciences I was responsible for ensuring that copy was written, produced, edited and published within strict turnaround times.

Being able to effectively highlight examples of how you meet key criteria is essential to being successful in the shortlisting process. In order to know what transferable skills to include in an application for a new role, it is a good idea to look at job postings that you might be interested in. This will allow you to prioritize the skills employers are looking for. It is especially important to use the same language that the employer is using and to include relevant descriptions of experience on your CV.

Now let us review some people-management vacancies across different sectors in order to examine how to frame transferable skills.

PEOPLE MANAGEMENT VACANCIES

HR performance management

What follows is an excerpt from a job vacancy in the UK public sector. Note the transferable skills (highlighted in bold) that you might have developed from previous work experience, perhaps as a line manager.

The role

With a passion for people management and a desire to build sound HR foundations, the postholder will work with the head of regional people service delivery and key stakeholders to optimize effective working relationships and ensure the maximum impact of HR on business effectiveness.

The role involves a proactive approach to **problem-solving** and enabling the business to find solutions to HR challenges. With a generalist knowledge of case management and essential functional HR experience, the role is key to enabling business leaders through the interpretation of HR policy, the application of case management advice and the delivery of key HR processes.

As the first point of contact to the business, the postholder will be required to **manage stakeholder expectations** and **gather business intelligence** to provide specialist advice or to deploy the appropriate service from within the team.

Key responsibilities

- **Analyse HR data** and apply understanding to decide on an appropriate intervention or course of action. Consider sensitive or multiple opposing opinions to establish facts, determine appropriate methodologies and find the best approach. Ensure the quality and application of results based on analysis.
- **Maintain team relationships** by supporting others, contribute to team decisions and use initiative to solve problems. Work with others to identify areas for improvement and simplify processes to use fewer resources.
- Clearly explain to colleagues the reasons for change and how to implement it, supporting individuals with different needs to adapt to change.
- **Take managed risks** by fully considering the varied impact changes could have on the diverse range of end users.
- **Communicate** in a straightforward, honest and engaging manner, choosing appropriate styles to maximize understanding and impact. Share information as appropriate and check understanding.

Note those highlighted words and terms: they are transferable skills that you may have developed, i.e. the ability to problem solve, manage stakeholders, maintain team relationships. Many of these skills are generic. You may have led a team previously, managed stakeholder expectations or analysed business data. What examples can you provide that demonstrate the skill set required for this role?

HR and compliance coordinator

In the following example both HR and compliance knowledge and skills are required. You might consider how your previous work and voluntary experience might prepare you for the responsibilities and requirements outlined below.

The role

The postholder is responsible for the efficient and effective day-to-day running of the charity, including providing support in delivering human resources, learning and development, health and safety, quality, compliance, and other administrative requirements.

Key responsibilities

- **Run organizational recruitment processes** from start to finish, including developing job descriptions, placing adverts on various websites, preparing shortlisting documents, arranging interviews, and ensuring candidates are appointed to post smoothly.
- Work alongside the senior leadership team (SLT) to develop and refine the organization's induction programme, including **developing new processes** and documentation to support thorough and bespoke inductions.
- **Implement the new induction programme** for all incoming staff members to ensure they settle into their roles and are given the support they need.
- **Respond to queries** and deal with applications from people who wish to volunteer.
- **Develop** an organizational HR **database** and improve the knowledge management processes, to ensure proper and **streamlined documentation** of all relevant staff records.
- **Identify and implement** relevant HR-related **software** to enable the organization to become more efficient and effective.

- Support the director of operations to **maintain an accurate record of contracts** for all staff, consultants and contractors.

Requirements

- Excellent understanding of **administration systems**
- Understanding of **legal compliance, data protection, safeguarding, and incident and risk management**
- Strong **stakeholder management experience** (both internal and external)
- IT literacy, competent user of **MS Office package** and experience of databases and data entry
- High levels of **confidentiality**, the ability to act with discretion, sensitivity and diplomacy

This role requires two skill sets: compliance and HR. If you have a background in financial services, law, quality assurance or related areas you may be well placed to meet the criteria for this role. You may also be able to evidence the skill requirements highlighted through voluntary experience, e.g. trustee work, administrative support and contract work. There is considerable scope for transferable skills in this position.

Talent acquisition specialist

The following role may suit someone with some recruitment or event campaign experience. When reading through the responsibilities and requirements you might take note of some examples from your own experience. This will help you in future job applications.

The role

As talent acquisition specialist you will work closely with business units to deliver a high-quality recruitment service in line with organizational business needs. Reporting to the head of talent acquisition, you will be a part of the global talent team responsible for end-to-end recruitment services. We are going through a positive transformation to make our ways of working smarter and we are looking for someone who will add value to both project and process improvements.

Key responsibilities

- Work with hiring managers to identify and design appropriate campaigns to continue building our talented and diverse teams.
- Take detailed recruitment briefs, ask incisive questions and rapidly build your organizational knowledge and understanding to add value at all stages of the recruitment process.
- Advise hiring managers on recruitment best practice and keep them and yourself up to date with market trends and legislation.
- **Communicate effectively and positively** with potential applicants and candidates, representing the organization as an employer of choice.
- Build a talent pipeline.
- **Provide accurate** recruitment, onboarding and employee **administration** including job descriptions and contracts.

Requirements

- Experience of working in a **fast-paced environment**, successfully delivering to multiple deadlines and **prioritizing your workload**
- Experience of **managing multiple stakeholders** at all levels of seniority
- Strong **planning and organizing skills**
- **Knowledge of HR systems** and processes
- The ability to work productively on a remote basis
- Demonstrable **commitment** to the principles of **diversity and inclusion**

When deciding which roles to apply for, pay attention to the specific words being used to increase your chances of selection. For example, does the role require knowledge of HR systems and processes (which you might have developed through line-management experience) or specific experience in a people professional role?

Top tip

When completing applications and compiling CVs, focus on the verbs being used, such as 'organized', 'produced', 'advised', 'delivered', 'established', 'managed', 'built', 'implemented'. Additionally, ensure that workplace examples fulfil the role criteria. What did *you* do?

THE PROFESSIONAL DEVELOPMENT AUDIT

A professional development audit is a systematic review of your existing skills, knowledge and experience. It is a written document that captures all the competencies you currently have and how advanced those abilities are. It can be helpful to discuss your audit with others – family, friends, work colleagues – so that you might be reminded of other skills, knowledge and experience you have. An audit is a live document rather than a one-off exercise, and it can be very useful in helping you identify gaps in your current competency set.

Perhaps you have a clear idea of your next intended career move or else a broad idea of your preferred career trajectory. Consider the strengths, skills and knowledge that you already possess that support your career aspirations. Follow the same process for your work experience. In which areas are you strong? Which elements do you need to focus on?

You might like to use an advertisement for a job role relevant to your career aspirations. The first thing to do is to write down all the competencies that you feel you have gained next to the job descriptions. Pay particular attention to job roles that you are interested in applying for. Review your experience levels critically in each area (you might find it useful to use a rating system from 1 (low) to 10 (high) to help you prioritize). This exercise helps you to determine your priority areas for development.

Using the template provided in table 9 below you might consider the extent to which you are doing well or need to improve against the compentencies listed. You can swap these competencies for those that you find in job specifications you are interested in and for which you would like to apply.

Table 9 Example professional skills audit.

Competencies	Rating 1–10	Doing well	Need to improve	Notes
Team working				
Stakeholder management				
Facilitation				
Consulting				
Coaching and mentoring				
Performance management				
Workforce planning				
Diversity and inclusion				
Regulation and law				
Policy development				
Well-being				
Commercial mindset				

If, having reviewed the HR positions above, you feel they are not quite right for you at this stage, you might perhaps consider similar roles that are not directly HR-related but that require comparable skills. These similar roles, such as those in recruitment or learning and development, could provide you with an opportunity for a sideways move.

BECOME A RECRUITER

A recruiter is someone who finds qualified candidates for a job opening and works to meet the demands of both the employer and the candidate throughout the hiring process. Note that there are many different types of recruiter: agency recruiters (for both temporary and permanent staff; sometimes referred to as staffing agencies), contingency recruiters (often specializing in niche roles), executive searchers (specializing in senior talent) and in-house recruiters (employed by organizations to resource in-house talent).

Over the years I have worked with many professionals who have traversed a path to the people profession through their recruitment experience. After all, the skills acquired in these roles provide a great fit for those required in people management. If you have particular expertise in sales and marketing, you may find that a horizontal move to recruiting for sales and marketing roles is a straightforward sidestep. The same can be applied to a wide range of positions: engineering, distribution, health, teaching, and so on.

The vacancy included below is a recruiter position for the IT profession.

Entry-level recruitment consultant

With offices spanning sixty locations across three continents, we specialize primarily in placing candidates with experience in Microsoft, Salesforce or AWS technology. To date we have placed over 60,000 candidates in businesses ranging from start-ups to global enterprise companies, and we pride ourselves on our ability to deliver the highest quality candidates on the market.

The role

As a recruitment consultant, your main goals are to develop relationships with clients who have technology staffing needs and to find and place highly skilled IT professionals in those positions. It is a **sales-driven role** where you put focus on building **strong relationships** with clients and candidates. When you join, we'll provide you with full training and all the mentoring you need to be successful.

You'll cover business development, client and candidate management, contract negotiation, business-to-business sales and recruitment best practices, enabling you to carry out the following.

Key responsibilities

- Source candidates proactively via LinkedIn, job boards, advertising, referrals and our internal database.
- Develop the business by seeking and building relationships with new and existing clients to identify new roles and opportunities.
- Manage the recruitment process by arranging job interviews, salary negotiation and closing to ensure the successful placement of your candidates.

Requirements

- Ambitious individuals with a proven track record of success. This could be through sports, extracurricular activities or sales roles
- Driven and resilient individuals with an ongoing desire to improve
- Fluency in written and spoken English

You will note that this vacancy does not require any specific previous work experience and full training is provided. Successful candidates are likely to be those who can demonstrate success in some activity outside of work or those who have gained some experience in an area of sales. Note the words highlighted above: the key here is to be able to quantify your success in sales or communication. For example, if you have sales experience, you might be able to discuss your success in terms of profitability or the increase in the number of customers or in customer satisfaction. To evidence your track record of success outside of work you might consider how many sporting events you won over a period of time or your rate of progress; alternatively, look to other notable achievements such as the Duke of Edinburgh award, music grades or volunteering. Being able to give evidence of your resilience and drive when pursuing a goal is one of the key criteria for success in this role.

Case study

Ralph swapped his career as an entertainer and dancer on cruise liners for a recruitment role specializing in the leisure and hospitality sector after he became tired of the constant travel. He was able to use his extrovert nature and outgoing personality to develop effective relationships with clients. He enjoys working autonomously and having a caseload of jobs to source, and he really loves sharing his stories of working aboard ships. It is a busy role with targets to meet but there is also flexibility and the chance to work remotely as and when required.

Talent acquisition specialist

This example is an internal resourcing role for an accounting organization. Rather than resourcing for a number of organizations, the role will focus on ensuring the right people are recruited to the right department at the right time. There does not tend to be much of a sales focus in these positions (other than marketing the organization to candidates).

The role

The talent acquisition specialist will conduct full-cycle recruiting for all experienced public accounting (tax and audit) and related candidates within their region. A typical day might include the following.

Key responsibilities

- Build relationships and communicate with hiring managers across the region to gather relevant information on their current recruiting needs as well as their future needs.
- Utilize a variety of tools, resources and networks to search for and find candidates who have the skill set and experience needed to fill openings (or anticipated future needs) across the region.
- Assist candidates through the full recruiting process to assure a best-in-class candidate experience. This includes interactions whilst sourcing candidates, conducting phone interviews, coordinating in-office interviews, organizing application paperwork and extending offers.
- Update information in the applicant tracking system to ensure compliance and regulatory guidelines are being met.
- Collaborate with other team members to improve and streamline recruiting processes.
- Attend recruitment-related events and functions, presenting the organization in a professional, enthusiastic manner.

Requirements

- **Tech-savvy** and the ability to learn new systems/software quickly

- **Strong communication** skills (both written and verbal)
- Enthusiasm for **building relationships** with hiring managers, recognizing the importance of keeping them updated regularly
- **Bachelor's degree in human resources, business administration or a relevant field, or equivalent experience**
- Familiar with and proficient in multiple candidate sourcing methods
- High professional standards, maintaining strict client confidentiality

If you have previously worked as a line manager where you gained experience in high-volume recruiting, you are likely to have acquired a sound background for applying for this position. However, you will note that having a degree in human resources, business administration or a related field may also position you effectively for the role. Consider the examples you might bring from other roles you have worked in to evidence your skills in communication and building relationships. For example, you might say:

> As a newly recruited manager in a new department I was required to identify the key strategic priorities of the organization and align my departmental strategic targets. This necessitated working closely with the executive team in gaining approval for my strategic plan and gaining the support of my colleagues in the senior management team. I achieved this though scheduling time to build relationships in my first month with the organization, finding out about the remit of each and how we could work effectively together.

Note also the requirement to be tech savvy. This refers to your knowledge of new technology and its ability to support you in your role. Therefore, it is about your aptitude to take advantage of technology to ensure that you manage processes more efficiently. Consider how technology has improved the efficiency and effectiveness of your performance in current or previous roles or during your studies.

As mentioned above, recruiting can be a great way to achieve a horizontal move into the people profession, allowing you to utilize previous skills and to build on these in your new position. This can help you to navigate a career in people management, but it is not the only way. You may prefer to explore a horizontal move through other roles such as a learning and development role.

LEARNING AND DEVELOPMENT

Learning and development roles provide an opportunity to create a culture of learning and growth in an organization. Learning and development professionals understand the strategic goals of the organization and assess future capability needs to meet the priorities of their organization. They implement learning initiatives to help individuals develop. This might include carrying out capability assessments, designing blended learning, designing learning interventions, facilitating learning, monitoring the effectiveness of learning, and more. A sideways step to learning and development is often possible for those with strong industry knowledge – whether that be in insurance, nursing or sales – and for those who wish to use this to develop others. Let us review two learning and development vacancies below.

Learning and development assistant

The role

This is an exciting new opportunity for a learning and development assistant to play an integral role in helping the learning and development team to deliver their learning and development strategy for the organization.

We are looking for candidates who are self-starting, able to build strong and lasting relationships and who are flexible in their approach. This role is extremely varied so the ability to be autonomous and hit the ground running is essential.

Key responsibilities

- Designing and delivering training
- Overseeing training programmes across the entire organization
- Liaising with stakeholders to understand training needs
- Acting as the point of contact for third-party suppliers
- Managing the learning management system in a timely, organized manner
- Regularly reviewing training programmes
- Arranging confidential coaching meetings
- Liaising and building relationships both internally and externally

Requirements

- Excellent accuracy and **attention to detail**
- Confidence **delivering training both online and in-person**
- Strong **working knowledge** of **learning and development**
- Experience working in a **professional services** environment
- Experience working with **learning management systems and e-learning**
- Strong IT skills in Word, Excel and PowerPoint

You will note that this role requires confidence in delivering both online and in-person training. You may have developed this in your current role through delivering staff inductions, coaching and mentoring colleagues, delivering webinars, and so on. Consider the aspects of your current role where you support new staff, conduct tours of the organization or train colleagues on specific software. If you do not yet have experience in this area but are interested in this kind of role, you might think about how you can find opportunities in your current role to develop key skills and knowledge.

In order to support the working-knowledge requirement in this role you might consider undertaking an entry-level qualification to fill any underpinning theory gaps you identify (see chapters 4 and 10). You might also have noticed a requirement for experience of working in a professional services environment. Professional services includes architects, accountants, engineers, doctors, lawyers, teachers, tax advisors, IT services and management advice.

Being competent in the use of technology will be beneficial in this role so you might want to think about how you use various platforms and systems to aid the efficiency of your work, to evaluate outcomes and reports and to communicate with stakeholders. Consider how technology has improved your life (having hundreds of available books on your Kindle; using WhatsApp to stay in touch with your team; organizing your time with a productivity app). Have you taught others to use technology? How did you do this and what was the outcome? Have you used technology to aid decision making? The key is not just to list your knowledge and skills but to give the recruiting team evidence of how you have applied them.

PITCHING YOUR APPLICATION

The level at which you might pitch your application for a new role will depend on your current skills, knowledge and experience. For those who have been working as line managers and can evidence effective people management skills, a horizontal move into an HR Business Partner or HR Manager role may be appropriate. For example, as a practitioner in a large international organization in the telecommunications and energy sector, I reported to a Director of HR who had achieved a sideways move from a regional manager position. For those with less experience, or perhaps for someone whose previous job roles have been significantly different, it may be appropriate to step down into an entry-level role for a while in order to gain experience.

Case study

Katrina had worked as a management consultant for some years and she had a broad knowledge of people management issues. However, she was keen to gain corporate experience, to update her skills in employment law and to develop knowledge of casework. She applied for roles as an HR advisor and was successfully appointed at a UK university. Her salary dropped by a third. Two years later she gained an HR manager role with a different university, having developed a broad range of HR generalist skills and knowledge. She is now searching for her next move to chief people officer.

OPPORTUNITIES IN YOUR WORKPLACE

Learning and development roles are more likely to exist in larger organizations, where the internal development function supports the organization in the delivery of its strategic plan, ensuring that staff are equipped with the skills and knowledge required to be successful in their roles. If a role is not available in your current workplace, there might still be opportunities to gain useful experience that would support future applications to roles in other organizations.

Case study

Lydia completed a degree in Spanish and French and then spent several enjoyable years travelling as a translator. On her return to the UK she found a part-time role as a teacher of languages in a small private training centre. She undertook teaching qualifications while in the role and then, after several years, she started to train new teachers. Lydia found she had a passion for teaching but was keen to progress her career in more of a corporate role. She was interested in pursuing a career as a learning and development professional in the private sector. Three years ago Lydia undertook the CIPD postgraduate diploma in human resource management. On completing the course she successfully secured a role as a learning and development advisor for a large IT organization.

An organization example

Early in my career, while working for BAE Systems in the UK, I designed and delivered a leadership programme for all those with leadership responsibility – from supervisors right up to the CEO. The programme consisted of two blocks of two days of classroom-based training. It involved a range of skills-based exercises, including role play, performance management, team-building, delegation, time management, communication audits, interviewing and other skills. In order to keep group sizes to a maximum of twelve I needed to expand the team of trainers. I recruited three aircraft engineers to support me, none of whom had any previous training experience. I arranged for each to undertake a 'train the trainer' programme in the first instance, followed by observation of the training delivery and mentoring. They were able to use their technical knowledge to underpin the training content, ensuring it was tailored to the needs of the participants. Two of them enjoyed the experience so much they decided to pursue a change of career, transferring to the HR function within the same organization.

SUMMARY

In this chapter we have explored multiple vacancies in the people profession in order to examine how existing skills and knowledge might be transferred to these roles. We have focused on key words in the person specification (the 'Requirements' sections) so that we are able to evidence our experience in alignment with key criteria. We have considered how a horizontal move to either recruitment or learning and development might provide an entry route into the people profession, so that existing specialist skills can be utilized and transferred to a specialist role in the people profession. The people profession will benefit from your previous work experience so now is your chance to reflect on your role preferences, your transferable skills and your job-application techniques.

Chapter 7

THE JOB SEARCH

WHETHER YOU ARE AT THE start of your career and seeking your first role or transitioning mid-career, this chapter should provide some good job-searching tips from specialist people management recruiters and career professionals. We explore how to prepare a CV and how to target specific vacancies, how to use photos and videos to support your application and how to find your ideal role through specialist platforms and agencies. We consider the power of networks in helping you secure a new role, and we look at how to foster those networks by connecting and developing relationships with old and new contacts. CV templates are provided for both generalist and specialist people-related roles.

PREPARING YOUR CV

Over the years I have placed adverts for numerous roles in people management, learning and development, leadership and management, and lecturing roles. I am always amazed at the number of people who send their CV through with little consideration of the advertised role. In some cases I wonder if the applicant has even read the job advertisement. When faced with a high volume of responses, recruiters simply do not have time to try to find some relevant experience in your application. Applications need to be clear and aligned with the job advertisement. Focus on making it as easy as possible for the recruiter to match your knowledge, skills and experience to the vacancy.

In the previous chapter we explored multiple people-related vacancies and the person specifications that detail the requirements of the role. Role expectations might be defined in terms of essential or desirable competencies. The example in table 10 provides a clear guide to the essential and desirable criteria required for an HR role; your CV needs to evidence as many of these criteria as possible to ensure that you are successful in getting to the next stage of the recruitment process.

Most people tend to create a generic CV and then amend this to suit the requirements of the role. However, you may need more than one generic CV if you are pursuing different kinds of role. For example, I have one CV for my academic work, one for my consultancy and one for my non-executive roles. Your CV needs to be accurate, truthful and verifiable as you will likely be asked to provide further details at the interview stage. Tailor your CV so that it aligns with the essential and desirable criteria as far as possible. Also, consider how you might evidence the specialist knowledge indicated above. For example, you may have studied employment legislation and/or attended professional training, which you used in a previous paid or voluntary role. The key is to reflect on examples that can cover multiple criteria. The following case study illustrates how you might evidence your knowledge and experience across several areas using just one example.

Case study

Ruberta has a passion for dinghy sailing and achieved her Royal Yachting Association dinghy instructor qualification 3 years ago. This training included a programme on 'safe and fun', which is a safeguarding course for those working with young people and vulnerable adults in a training environment. Ruberta uses this

Table 10 Example person specification for an HR Manager role in a large school in the UK.

Essential	Desirable
Qualifications	
First degree or experience that demonstrates equivalent level of knowledge and skills	Other management qualification
CIPD chartered status (MCIPD) minimum	
Evidence of relevant continuous professional development	
Experience	
Experience in an HR generalist role, providing proactive and solutions-focused advice to managers and staff	Experience of working within the education sector and in particular an independent school
Experience of dealing with casework (e.g. disciplinary, grievance, capability, absence)	Previous experience of managing an HR function
Experience of developing and improving the delivery of HR processes	Experience of leading and managing organizational change
Specialist knowledge	
An up-to-date knowledge of employment legislation	ISI compliance requirements
Safer Recruitment and safeguarding	
Personal qualities	
Customer-focused	
Passionate about the contribution HR can make to the school	
Able to maintain a high degree of confidentiality	
Able to work on own initiative	
Able to influence and persuade by building credibility, respect and support with colleagues	
Clear, concise and influential communication skills	
Strong commitment to equality and diversity	

education and her experience as an instructor to highlight her knowledge of safeguarding. She is also able to use her teaching experience to evidence her commitment to equality and diversity, her communication skills, initiative and her customer-focused approach.

WHAT MAKES A GOOD CV

Last year I advertised a learning and development post for a small training organization in London. I received more than 100 applications. According to Glassdoor, each corporate job is likely to attract more than 250 CVs. Of those candidates, between four and six are likely to get called for interview, and only one will get the job.[23] In my experience, the number of applicants depends on the geographical region, the nature of the role and the salary offered. Generally, recruiters spend little time sifting CVs for match and non-match criteria. According to Reed, recruiters spend as little as 7 seconds on your CV, and increasingly the first scan might be made by a computer programme or an applicant tracking system.[24] Those initial seconds really do count, therefore. This is why it is so important to tell recruiters why you are the best person for the role. Focus on the ways in which you are unique. It is not just about what you do, but who you are. Wherever possible, include quantifiable data that support your claims. Avoid saying things like 'I managed three events a year' and instead include details on how many people your events targeted, the contribution of your role and the successful outcome. Good practice in CV writing differs according to personal preference. There is no set format. However, the following key areas are non-negotiable.

- Your CV needs to be accurate, so pay attention to spelling and grammar.
- Keep it simple and concise. Avoid jargon and do not exceed three pages (maximum).

- Ask a trusted colleague, friend or relative to proofread your final draft prior to submission.
- You will need to include your name and contact details (email address and phone number). You may include a link to your LinkedIn profile if you use this platform (see below). A date of birth is not required.
- Create a short personal statement at the beginning of your CV to sell yourself. This should include details of your skills, experience and personal qualities. Tailor this statement to the requirements of the job.
- Include achievements and provide evidence of how targets were exceeded, projects managed and outcomes ensured. Remember, recruiters are interested in quantifiable data.

The structure of your CV should be as follows.

Personal statement

Example: 'Dependable people professional with more than 3 years' experience in companies with more than 10,000 employees. CIPD qualified to level 5, achieving CIPD student of the year award in 2020. Cut costs by £40,000 monthly by implementing an applicant tracking system. Seeking to use knowledge of high-volume recruiting to become a people business partner at Madeup Solutions Ltd.'

Work experience

Start with your most recent role and include your job title and the name of the organization plus a little context. For example: 'Madeup Solutions Ltd is the largest producer of tennis balls in Europe, employing 40,000 staff.' Include your time in post ('from December 2018 to present') and your key responsibilities.

Achievements

Focus here on how your experience to date prepares you for the role you are applying for. Why are you the best candidate for the role? List your skills and achievements and support them with examples. Think about quantifiable achievements: what did I do, and, so what? For example: 'I created a new onboarding programme for the division of my company and 100% of divisions adopted this as good practice.'

Education

Include qualifications that you have achieved along with the relevant dates. You may wish to emphasize the qualifications that are most relevant to the role. If you have more educational achievements than work experience, you may wish to prioritize this section.

Hobbies and interests

It is only necessary to include hobbies and interests if it helps you to stand out from the crowd. Focus on what will genuinely add value to your CV.

You will find two example CVs in figures 4 and 5 on the following pages. The first is a short CV designed by a recent graduate. It includes details of work experience, education and voluntary work. The second is a little longer and presents the work experience and education for a mid-career people professional. Note that the applicant's current experience is provided in detail whereas other roles are just summarized. Remember that recruiters will only skim-read your CV so it is important that it is concise while including all relevant points.

Both CV examples include 'References on request'. An employer will ask for references if they decide to proceed with your application so it is not necessary to provide details at this stage.

Compiling a CV takes time. Once you have drafted your first version, leave it for a day or two and then revisit it. Consider whether it

Arianna Mundley

Email: amundley@rhyta.com LinkedIn: linkedin.com_amundge Phone: 1234 567 8943

A motivated, adaptable and responsible human resource management graduate seeking a position in talent acquisition, which will utilize the professional and people management skills developed through previous work experience in this area. I have strong interpersonal and customer-facing competencies and the drive to see things through to completion. In my current role I have managed the candidate experience from advertisement to onboarding for over twenty roles of varying levels of seniority.

Achievements

- Association member of the Chartered Institute of Personnel Development gained through completion of certificate in people practice
- Employee of the month award in recognition of contribution to the candidate experience

Education

Oct 2016–June 2020 BA (Hons) Human Resource Management London Metropolitan University

- People and organizations
- International business
- Resourcing talent
- Digital organizations

Aug 2014–July 2016 A levels Ranbury College
Grades achieved: Maths, B; Economics, B; Psychology, A

Employment

June 2020–present HR Assistant MadeupUK Ltd

Key responsibilities:

- First point of contact for all internal staff face-to-face, online and via telephone
- Directing managers to organizational policies and procedures
- Assisting the HR team with all aspects of the employee lifecycle with a focus on resourcing talent
- Coordinating the onboarding process and communicating with all stakeholders
- Departmental expert in SAP Analytics, social media and data reporting

Hobbies and interests

Volunteer steward for the Covid-19 vaccination programme

References

Available on request

Figure 4 Example CV for a recent graduate working with first role experience.

is a fair representation of your skills, knowledge, achievements and experience. Does it read well? What else might you add? When it is complete it is necessary to revisit it every time you apply for a new role. A common mistake people make is just to add their latest role to the top of their CV, meaning that after a few roles the document

Fiona Smith
12 Millery Close, London, SW13 5FK
Mobile: 07986582234 Home: 020 3323 4567 LinkedIn: SmithF_linkedin.com

Executive summary

A business/human resources consultant with a track record of working strategically to support organizational objectives. Key strengths include creating employee engagement, well-being and learning and development programmes to improve corporate communication, thus increasing staff retention and reducing sickness absence. Designed and delivered effective coaching and mentoring programmes that are low cost yet effective. Strong presentation skills, with extensive experience in addressing the board and delivering briefings, speaking at conferences and delivering both training programmes and seminars that genuinely deliver results. Deep knowledge of resourcing talent, employment law and organization development, gained through projects and experience in the public and private sector.

Career highlights

- Set up the corporate development department from scratch at City College Norwich and University of Suffolk. Recruited staff, undertook a corporate learning needs analysis in relation to strategic objectives, developed a learning and development programme and a leadership development programme. Managed a core team of six people, along with departmental budgets and consultants. Accredited a range of programmes with national awarding bodies and sold these to external clients in order to fund additional opportunities for staff.
- Developed a collaborative coaching and mentoring programme with public sector organizations across Suffolk, Norfolk and Essex. Trained all staff centrally, ensuring a pool of available coaches. Set up a matching service to support the appointment and management of both coaches and mentors across organizations. Investment was minimal but the rewards were significant in terms of sharing good practice, encouraging creativity and supporting talent development.

Career history

Employer: New Hope College
Position: People Development Manager
Dates: May 2012–November 2021

- Developed learning and development strategy and set up corporate development department. Recruited and managed team, budget, consultants and external trainers.
- Developed and facilitated 'our culture' workshops with senior managers to establish key values and how to promote these in support of organization growth targets. Appointed 'change champions' in each department and facilitated focus groups to promote effective communication in a period of rapid growth. Worked directly with the CEO/provost in identifying leadership development needs to support strategic objectives.
- Developed and implemented performance management policy, system and training. Increased performance development review completion rates from 40% to 100% in 18 months.
- Worked with heads of departments to identify and manage resourcing needs, developed succession plan to support organization's strategic goals. Managed assessment centres and development centres for the promotion of key staff.
- Implemented flexible benefits programmes and health and well-being strategy. Reduced sickness absence from 6.5% to 4%.
- Developed policy, committee and development programmes to support the university equality and diversity agenda. Conducted audit as a tool for action planning across the institution with community partners.
- Implemented and managed employee attitude survey through the *Sunday Times* 100 Best Companies quality standard. Used KPIs to support staff retention, designed and implemented events to support strategic plan.
- Led on internal communications, facilitated focus group to support consultative process, worked with trade unions to support effective change management. Created the annual staff recognition awards.

Earlier career

- 2009–2012: City College Norwich, Corporate Development, Equality and Diversity Manager
- 2005–2009: Pirelli Cables, National Graduate Recruitment and Development and HR Advisor
- 2003–2005: GEC Alsthom Transport, Learning and Development Advisor
- 2001–2003: BAE Systems, Organization Development Advisor

Voluntary experience

- 2018–present: school governor at Littleton First School
- 2017–present: sailing instructor for Youth Advance

Figure 5 Example CV for experienced people professional with experience in multiple roles.

Education and memberships

- MA HRM
- MEd Training and Development
- PGCE
- BA (Hons) Business
- Member status of the CIPD
- Professionally accredited for the UK register of career coaches
- ILM Level 5 Coaching and Mentoring
- BPS Level A and B

References

Available on request

Figure 5 Continued.

becomes too large. You need to ensure that your experience is tailored to the role that you are applying for.

Be cautious of using gimmicks to stand out from the crowd. Over the years I have received documents sprayed with perfume, ones that were printed on bright coloured paper or attached with ribbons. The biggest contention of all is over whether to include a photo or picture. There is no right or wrong answer here so do what you feel most comfortable with. Some people love them and some people loathe them.

THE VIDEO CV

The latest idea in recruitment is to support your CV with a video. A short video (1–3 minutes) enables you to provide real insight into you rather than just following a standardized approach. Video CVs are more commonly used in creative and customer-facing roles in sectors such as advertising, creative arts, marketing, media and PR, but they are increasingly being introduced in other fields and I am sure it will not be too long before many of us are required to compile videos in support of our CVs.

While making a video will cause anxiety for some, for others it provides an opportunity to take the role of interviewee using a medium that can be erased if it fails to produce your intended results. If you are tasked with making a video, do think about the format. Will you simply talk to the camera or will you ask someone to interview you? Think about what you will say prior to pressing record. Compile a script (but do not read from it!) that prompts you to include key areas and a few clear phrases. Important considerations include *where* you will film: consider background noise, lighting and the position of your camera. There is nothing worse than being able to see only half of your face! Will you use your phone or a camera to record the video? Look back over what you produce to check for hesitancy or awkward moments. This is as important as proofreading your CV, so do edit the video if required. The video provides you with the opportunity to stand out from the crowd so try to display your personality, demonstrate your key skills and be creative. Consider the following things that employers are usually looking for.

- Include an introduction, a main section and a summary, and answer the question, 'Why are you the right person for the job?'
- Include your unique selling points: skills, experience and examples of your work experience.
- Make the video interesting! Include different scenes and let your personality shine through.

If video recording and editing is not your core strength, then ask a friend for assistance. You could help them with their CV writing in return!

THE COVERING LETTER

I often get asked if it is necessary to include a covering letter in addition to a CV. The answer is *always* yes! It is so important to write a convincing covering letter to introduce the core elements of your CV, to detail why you are interested in the role, and to engage the recruiter so that they will read your CV. The key is not to repeat what you have written in your CV but instead to summarize your core skills and experience.

An effective structure might include the following elements.

- Name and address. Include the name of the hiring manager.
- Opening paragraph: tailor the letter to the job application.
- The body: highlight your major achievements and how they relate to the vacancy.
- Closing paragraph: outline the next steps in the recruitment process.
- Close: use a formal salutation:, 'Yours sincerely', for example.

An example of a good covering letter is shown in figure 6 overleaf. It clearly relates to the person specification and highlights the key skills and experience required for the role. It should be no longer than one page of A4 paper.

COMPETENCY STATEMENTS

Some organizations will require you to evidence certain competencies in your application. You are likely to include these in your covering letter. Competencies might include things like those in the following examples.

- Customer focus: striving for high customer satisfaction, going out of your way to be helpful and pleasant, making it as easy as possible for the customer rather than the HR department or the university.
- Communication: balancing listening and talking, speaking and writing clearly and accurately, influencing others, keeping others informed.

30 June 2021

Bluebell Cottage
12 Wilson Way
Croydon
London
SW12 5TF

Dana Jinmba
Talent Manager
Ruemental Holdings Plc
London
NW45 8SL

Dear Ms Jinmba

Re: Vacancy for Leadership Development Manager

I would like to express my interest in the above position, advertised through Totaljobs, 29 June 2020.

I have 15 years of corporate development experience gained in both the public and private sectors, managing teams of between three and ten people and departmental budgets. Specifically, working with the board to identify strategic goals, I have designed, managed and delivered talent management programmes for Blanket Systems, BNB Foods, University of Springfold and City Museum Rothfield. This has included the management of national graduate and apprenticeship programmes. Much of my work experience has been project-based, including the following: implementation of Investors in People (IiP), the business excellence review, employee values surveys, the delivery of health and well-being strategies, regional and collaborative coaching, mentoring programmes and succession planning. I am currently working on a project to deliver apprenticeships for employers with Aspire Learning.

I have compiled and won bids for European social funding and the Learning and Skills Council, and I have managed projects to budget and time (study buddy programme, BME 16–18 aspirations). I am committed to continuing professional development: I have undertaken significant development annually in support of sector changes (e.g. quality assurance, assessor qualifications) and in support of good practice in succession planning, employment law and public sector duties.

I am a member of the Chartered Management Institute (CMI) and the British Academy of Management (BAM) and I have achieved a fellowship with the Institute of Leadership Development. These networks provide essential updates in all areas of leadership development.

I attach my CV for your information and, should this be of interest, I look forward to hearing from you.

Yours sincerely,

Rebecca Rounted

Figure 6 Example covering letter.

- Collegiality: being helpful, respectful, approachable and team-oriented, building strong working relationships and a positive work environment.

- Initiative: taking ownership of your work, doing what is needed without being asked, following through.
- Efficiency: planning ahead, managing time well, being on time, being cost-conscious, thinking of better ways to do things.

Competencies will differ across organizations so do check what is required for each specific role advertised. A copy of the relevant competency framework should be included with the job advert. You may be able to use examples from outside of your work life, such as your volunteering experience. Focus on what you personally did, the positive results (or lessons learned) and the impact on the business or on other people. Where possible, cross-reference to other skills required in the job specification. It is not sufficient to simply say that you have experience: you need to give evidence of how you have used that experience successfully.

The acronym STAR can be useful in helping you structure your statements effectively.

- S: situation. Set the scene and provide context for your example. Be specific and include names and dates where possible.
- T: task. Outline the task. What was your personal role? What were the major tasks required to resolve the situation?
- A: action. What did you actually *do* to resolve the situation? What steps did you take to ensure a successful outcome? Reinforce the skills required in the advert.
- R: result. What was the outcome? How can you quantify this?

Let us look at some examples.

- Situation: 'Last year, at the beginning of the Covid-19 pandemic, it became clear we would need to shut the office and arrange for staff to work from home. We had one week to achieve this.'

- Task: 'My role was to contact each of our fifty staff members to communicate the need to work from home and to find out what people would require immediately to be able to work effectively.'
- Action: 'I compiled an equipment list including laptops, screens, desks, chairs, and so on, and then worked with the relevant departments to ensure that items were purchased and delivered within the week. I also liaised with IT to ensure that all staff would be able to log into their emails and files remotely. I asked staff to check this while we were still in the office to eliminate any problems.'
- Result: 'I ensured that all staff had the right equipment in place within a week and this was delivered to their homes. Staff were able to log into their emails and access their files successfully from day one of homeworking.'

FINDING VACANCIES

There are many platforms and organizations that support you in identifying your ideal people-related role. Before we look at them, though, a quick tip: do ensure your CV is up to date and tailored to the vacancy before you apply!

LinkedIn

No matter what your previous work experience is or where you are in your career, a great place to start your job search is via LinkedIn. This platform enables you to stand out professionally as well apply for jobs directly.

The first thing to do is to create a profile. You can do this at the very beginning of your career, even while you are still a student. I have seen some really fantastic profiles of students, including their voluntary experience and university roles: editor of the student magazine, for example, or sports club events organizer. LinkedIn offers some great advice on how to create a professional profile. You can use the platform to display the courses you have completed, the languages you speak and the certifications you have gained. The key point here is that LinkedIn is both a job-searching platform and a networking platform, connecting you to people in a similar way to Facebook. When you develop your professional network, you will be 'linked in' with people who may be able to help you find a job.

Your professional profile provides you with an opportunity to showcase your expertise, skills and aspirations.[25] Complete all the required sections and make sure that you are visible to recruiters by letting them know you are open to opportunities (i.e. enable the #opentowork feature). Be active: build relationships with your connections by commenting on their posts. When you are ready you can send posts yourself so that you grow your visibility and remind your connections that you are there and available for work.

Professional bodies

The larger specialist HR management professional bodies include specialist sections for HR jobs. At the time of writing, the Society for Human Resource Management[26] is listing more than 1,500 jobs and the CIPD's 'PM Jobs' site is listing 409 roles.[27] The advantage of using job sites from professional bodies is that you will find a large number of relevant people professional roles in one place. You will be able to search for specialist vacancies across all levels of seniority, and the sites are likely to list only live vacancies (remember to watch closing dates and ensure that you apply in good time). Even if you do not find your ideal role on your first search, regular browsing of these jobs sites will give you an idea of what employers are looking for and will help you develop your skills and knowledge in alignment with your ideal job.

Other platforms

There is no shortage of sites that list relevant people management vacancies – check out sites such as www.indeed.com, www.monster.co.uk and www.totaljobs.com. A simple search for jobs in people management, HR, learning and development or similar roles will reveal plenty of opportunities. The key here, though, is to notice when the jobs were listed and to check they are still current. Do look for the closing date as recruiters are unlikely to accept applications after a deadline has passed (except where very few applications have been received). A word of caution: it is very easy to send multiple applications via these platforms but remember that the usual guidance applies. That is, do include a covering letter and do ensure that any application is tailored to the job vacancy. You only have a few seconds to make an impression before being dropped into the reject pile so make those moments count. Invest a little more time now for a better chance of success later.

Specialist recruitment agencies

Over the years I have worked with numerous specialist HR recruitment agencies. Generally, the overall experience is dependent on the recruiter that you work with and their experience in the marketplace. Smaller agencies can offer a personalized service where they really get to know you so that the jobs they send through are tailored to your needs. In some agencies the sheer volume of candidates that they are managing negatively affects the candidate experience, and you may find your CV put forward for jobs that are not aligned effectively with your skills and experience. Remember that recruitment consultants are generally paid by the employer who is seeking to fill a vacancy. Try to build a relationship with a recruiter so that they are aware of what you are seeking rather than just being familiar with your CV. You can make contact with recruiters via LinkedIn.

The power of networks

Building a network is one of the very best ways of securing your ideal role. Attending professional association meetings, breakfast clubs, conferences, seminars and any other events that provide the potential for meeting others in your chosen field is a great investment of your time. You will likely hear about roles before they are advertised and you will learn about the recruiting manager and what they are seeking. You may glean insights into the organization, its culture, vision and mission so that you are able to assess if it is right for you. You may even benefit from an introduction via your network.

In 2020 *Forbes* reported that between 70% and 80% of jobs are never even posted. This is what is termed the hidden job market, and it can be very difficult to break into without a powerful network. Even when jobs are advertised, perhaps due to an organization's policy, many recruiters will also send the link to their networks to encourage applications from people who they have worked with previously – candidates they know and trust.

As well as meeting people through peer-to-peer networking and professional groups, consider high-profile individuals who might be able to help you raise your visibility. Engaging a mentor is a great start and you may be able to do this through a professional body, a university or a business networking group.

Case study

More than a decade ago I met a colleague who was senior to me and she suggested a coffee one lunchtime. It was a great opportunity to bounce ideas around, navigate organizational politics and learn about managing at a senior level. We still meet up, many years after we both left the organization. I always consult my mentor when I am thinking about a new role or opportunity and she has provided many references for me. As I have progressed in my career, I have managed to help my mentor too, through introductions for consultancy assignments and opportunities for raising visibility through public speaking engagements.

Building networks is a long-term endeavour. It is about developing relationships that will support you in your career and not just your next role.

Recruiter advice

Alistair Stirling of Stirling Careers Consultancy has been advising clients on careers for many years.[28] Here is some of his advice:

> Attend webinars and use the chat box facility to network so that you can build on and share details of your knowledge and skills. Research the type of organization that you would like to work in and set up email alerts. Register with recruitment agencies too. Make sure you have a good CV and covering letter to send to employers and tailor each CV to the role that you are applying for. Then network, network, network!

SUMMARY

A significant section of this chapter has been dedicated to preparing applications, ensuring CVs are tailored to the vacancy, and exploring competency frameworks. Preparation is essential to ensuring that an initial application is converted to an interview offer. Job seekers too often focus their efforts on applying for multiple vacancies rather than crafting a good application. It takes time to respond to a vacancy effectively, but the more effort you invest in the early stages, the higher the conversion rate from application to interview. Once you have a CV that you are happy with, there are multiple ways in which to pursue your ideal role:

direct applications to companies, applying through one of the many job platforms, or using specialist recruitment agencies. Networking is a powerful way to let people know you are searching for a new role. Do not be shy: communicate your aspirations and ideal role with everyone who will listen.

Chapter 8

INTERVIEWS AND SELECTION TESTS

PREPARING FOR AN INTERVIEW IS a vital part of the job search process, and it entails much more than deciding what to say and how to present yourself. This chapter provides top tips for making a good impression, starting with research to find out more about the organization and the job role. Getting to know the organization – its vision, mission, strategic objectives and values – can help candidates prepare potential questions that can be asked at the end of the interview. Interview techniques, competency-based questions, psychometric testing and different employer approaches are also discussed here. The process of longlisting, shortlisting, first, second and subsequent interviews, alongside presentations and other selection tests, are explained with examples and case studies.

INTERVIEWS

You have been invited to interview: congratulations! Making it through to this stage means that a recruiter was sufficiently impressed by your application to find out more. This is a great start. The longlist stage is where the recruiter screens your application against the set criteria to ensure that you have the right to work legally in the country where the job exists and that you possess the essential requirements, such as professional qualifications. If there have been multiple good applications, you may be asked to a first assessment stage. This might involve presenting to an interview panel, a department or a group of stakeholders and/or undertaking psychometric/aptitude tests (see below).

Let us assume that you have made it to the shortlist: a small number of the very best applicants ranked according to their experience, skills, qualifications and competencies. The number of candidates invited to interview will differ according to the policy of the organization, the preference of the hiring manager and the number of applicants that meet the selection criteria. According to Glassdoor, an average of between four and six candidates are usually invited to interview; the recruitment corporation Jobvite suggests that one in six candidates will be called to interview.[29] In my experience, it really depends on whether an applicant meets the selection criteria. There have been occasions when I only interviewed one candidate, because they were the only applicant who met all the criteria, but generally four to six candidates provide a good pool from which to hire. Interviews are time-consuming and require a considerable investment of the hiring manager's time. This is why it is only possible to interview the very best candidates.

Reply promptly

You are most likely to receive your invitation to interview via email. Do check your inbox regularly and reply promptly. A growing number of organizations are using dedicated recruitment platforms to manage their recruiting process. This means that you may be directed to specific dates and times from which you can select your preferred option. If at all possible, choose one of the times provided, but if none of the available times are suitable it may be possible to request an alternative date. Note, though, that this is likely to be after other interviews are completed. Not all organizations offer this flexibility.

The challenge for recruiting teams is coordinating the busy diaries of hiring managers. Also, it is good practice to interview as a panel (see below), further complicating the juggling of convenient dates and times for interview.

Preparation

Having confirmed your interview arrangements, it is now time to prepare. There are several things to consider here.

The organization

Explore the website of the organization in greater detail (assuming you did this prior to your application). What are its vision, mission, strategic objectives and values? Has the organization been in the news at all (international, national or local, depending on its size)? What projects has the organization recently completed? Consider the sector the organization is working in: what are the challenges and opportunities? Also consider its main competitors. Undertaking this research demonstrates that you are interested in the organization and not just the role.

The role and potential interview questions

Read the job description, the person specification, the competency framework (if included) and any other accompanying information posted with the vacancy. It is likely that interview questions will be designed in alignment with this material so it is a good idea to study what the role requires.

Exploring possible interview questions in advance and thinking through some great examples will really help you to stand out from the competition. Practise answering questions based on the essential criteria that are included in the job advertisement. Here are some examples.

- 'Can you tell us a little about what attracted you to the role?' (Link your experience to the job profile.)
- 'Can you give me an example of when you managed a project to a tight budget and timeframe?' (Discuss a project that allows you to demonstrate your ability to manage a budget and schedule.)
- 'Can you tell me about a time when you were faced with managing conflict within a team?' (Consider examples from your work and/or voluntary experience with a specific focus on your role in managing a conflict.)

Using the STAR acronym – as discussed in chapter 7 – can help you structure your answers: situation, task, action, result. CAR – for context, action, review – is a similarly useful framework here, allowing you to demonstrate your experience. For example, if you were asked the question 'Can you give me an example of a time when you have handled a crisis?', you could go through the steps below.

- *Context.* 'I was a dinghy instructor delivering a programme for children between 11 and 14 years old. The group had some dinghy experience and I was teaching them how to advance their skills and prepare for club racing. Just as we were coming to the end of a session the weather changed suddenly, it became very windy and five of the eight boats capsized. I counted the heads of all the crew in the water and found that one of the dinghies had overturned and the crew were stuck underneath.'
- *Action.* 'I was concerned about everyone in the water but I needed to prioritize the boat where the children were stuck. I called the shore for help and asked for additional rescue boats to be launched. I asked my driver to keep the rescue boat steady next to the dinghy where the crew were trapped. I spoke calmly to the children, checked to see if they were OK and asked them to follow my instructions carefully. I reassured them while

arranging for the dinghy to be pulled up. In the meantime, I was overseeing the checking of all other dinghies to ensure that all crew were able to right their boats and get back onboard.'

- *Review*. 'All crew were successfully reinstated on their boats and the group was led to shore with less sail so that they arrived safely back and in control. Having experienced shore crew is essential in situations such as this.'

Interviewers will be recording your responses against the criteria in a standard form. Following the STAR or CAR frameworks enables you to demonstrate your experience and makes it easy for the interviewer to align your responses with the criteria.

Top tip

It is a good idea to prepare a couple of examples for each of the competencies defined for the role.

What else would you like to know about the role that is not included in the information you already have? Here are five questions you might ask at an interview.

- 'Are there opportunities for training and development within the organization?' (This provides an insight into how committed the organization is to the ongoing development of its staff.)
- 'What would a typical week in the role look like?' (This is a great question for establishing the variety of tasks involved, the stakeholders you might engage with, the degree of autonomy you might have, whether travel is a key part of the role, and so on.)
- 'How does the role support the organization's strategy?' (This emphasizes your business-partnering focus and will provide an idea of how your role aligns with the strategic goals of the organization.)

- 'What are the key performance indicators for the role?' (This question shows that you understand metrics and that you are keen to know how your performance will be measured.)
- 'How would you [the interviewer] describe the culture of the organization?' (This is one of my favourite questions as it can provide real insights into an organization, its people and its focus. I might follow up with 'What keeps you awake at night?' to assess the challenges ahead.)

Top tip

Ensure that your responses highlight what *you* have done – use 'I' rather than 'we'. If you are using a team example, do be careful to emphasize your role.

The interview

It is good practice for hiring managers to interview in a panel so that a wider perspective is provided. This helps to overcome issues of bias. This is the reason why interviewers use standardized questions, take notes, follow an interview guide and grade candidates on a rubric. Panel interviewers are likely to include the hiring manager and their colleagues and/or a member of the people team. As you are likely to be applying for a role in the people department, you will probably see a people professional on the panel. This might be the chief people officer or similar but that will depend on the seniority of the role and the size of the organization. A panel might include only two interviewers but can certainly include more.

Top tip

When responding to interview questions make eye contact with each of the panel members rather than just the interviewer asking the questions.

Interviews might be conducted in person or online, or there might be a mix of both depending on whether the organization includes multiple interviews during the selection process. All interviews should follow a similar four-part structure – the acronym WASP is useful here – as indicated below.

Welcome

The first part will be the welcome stage, where interviewers introduce themselves and confirm the format of the interview, including when you will have the opportunity to ask questions. At this stage the panel might provide further context for the vacancy and why it has arisen and tell you a little about the organization, its goals and the people.

Acquire information

This is the part where the interviewing panel will ask you questions related to the person specification and role competencies.

Supply information

This is your opportunity to ask questions. Take advantage of this time by having some questions prepared based on the research that you have undertaken. This demonstrates to the panel that you are genuinely interested in the role rather than just searching for a job.

Part

In the final part of the interview the panel will most likely confirm next steps, i.e. details of the next stage of the interview process, including information about a second interview if this is appropriate. They may wish to check your contact details in case of any changes, and they should let you know when you will be advised of their decision.

Preparing for face-to-face interviews

Hopefully you will now have undertaken research so that you are familiar with the organization, the sector it is in, and its competitors, clients, products and services. Another area you might research is the background of the interviewers, their roles and remits, the lengths of time they have been with the organization and their interests. This will be useful for when you are considering your questions.

It is a good idea to practise travelling to the organization prior to your interview so that you can work out how long it will take you to get there. Review train/bus timetables if required, book a taxi, explore the length of the drive time. If the interview is some distance from your current home, you might consider overnight accommodation, the location of nearby eateries and whether the organization will pay your interview expenses (this is becoming much less common).

Consider what you are going to wear at least several days prior to the interview so that you have time to purchase any items you might need. You might wish to explore the organization's dress code or contact the HR department. You need to feel comfortable during your interview, but you must also ensure that your clothes are in good condition. Avoid your favourite pair of ripped jeans, for example, and steer clear of wearing anything too revealing.

For a formal dress code it is important to wear a suit. Dark shoes that are polished work well. Keep jewellery simple and avoid any garment that is too distracting: the focus of the interviewers should be on what you are saying rather than on what you are wearing!

Just before the interview you may wish to practise some questions with family and friends and to remind yourself of any notes you have made about the organization.

Preparing for online interviews

Rather than needing to focus your efforts on finding the interview venue, the key to a successful online interview is your environment.

Where will you position yourself to avoid distraction and ensure you are not interrupted? Ensure your background is professional. Try to position yourself so your head and shoulders are displayed effectively and you are not too near or too far from the camera. Check which platform the organization will use for the interview and make sure you know how to use it (practise with friends and family on the same platform prior to the interview). Ensure you have received the link to the session in good time and diarize the time and date.

It is just as important to consider your attire when an interview is online as when it is in person. Dressing appropriately puts you in the right frame of mind and tells the interviewer(s) that you are taking the interview seriously. Eye contact and body language need to be emphasized when you are being interviewed online: look at the webcam to make eye contact with the interviewers. Nodding will show the interviewer that you are listening and engaged. Smile and sit up straight.

Consider a backup plan if the technology fails. Perhaps you might revert to the telephone or reschedule.

Responding to questions

For both in-person and online interviews it is important to respond effectively to the questions posed. Using STAR and CAR, as discussed above, will help you provide full responses. The key is to give the hiring team enough information and to gauge how long to talk for. Some interviewees, when nervous, talk too much so that the interviewer has to intervene to move them on. Practising with family and friends beforehand can help you to plan your responses.

SELECTION TESTS

In order to find out more about you, employers may ask you to complete a selection test as part of your application. Selection tests are a useful addition to aid decision making because they are objective, generally represent good value, and they can test a variety of elements. There are many organizations that offer selection tests and they are likely to use the services of an external specialist such as SHL to support their selection process. SHL provides a number of practice tests on their website, allowing you to become familiar with question types prior to the event.[30] You may be asked to take a test before your first interview or ahead of a second interview. Selection tests take different forms but might include any of the following.

Motivation questionnaires

Hiring managers will be keen to find out what drives you to perform well at work. They might focus on circumstances that encourage you to work harder and those that might demotivate you.

Example

Rate each of the following statements in relation to how it would affect your motivation at work. Choose the appropriate option out of A–E, with A being 'greatly reduces my motivation to work' and E being 'greatly increases my motivation to work'.

- Being expected to take responsibility for tasks
- Being required to train colleagues

Interest inventories

These are used to assess your preferences and opinions on a variety of different activities. The tool is used to discover your preferences for working with people, projects, numbers, and so on.

Simulation exercises

These exercises are used to assess the skills you will need on the job. You could be provided with an 'in tray' of typical tasks that you might be required to perform and be asked to prioritize them. You might be asked to take part in a role play, which assesses skills in areas such as negotiation and managing conflict.

Psychometric testing

Psychometric tests include both personality-based assessments and aptitude tests. Personality tests might measure motivation and work behaviour, for example. Aptitude tests could include numerical and verbal reasoning, logical reasoning (testing logical problem-solving ability) and critical thinking (testing analytical ability). There is a large body of evidence showing that psychometric tests are a good indicator of future performance.

Example: critical-thinking question

The red bus stops every 10 minutes.
The green bus stops every 20 minutes.
Both buses stop at Clapgate Lane.
The red bus has twice as many stops as the green bus.
The two buses never stop at the same time.

- The last statement is true.
- **There is insufficient data to tell whether it is true or false.**
- The last statement is false.

The correct answer is in bold.

If you are asked to complete a psychometric test, it is a good idea to practise first. This will provide you with an idea of the structure and how to manage the time available. Psychometric tests are more likely to be used for graduate and senior leadership positions.

Presentations

Asking candidates to undertake a timed presentation is common practice in the people profession. First, be clear about the theme for the presentation and the time allocation, and then develop a clear structure.

Tell them what you are going to tell them

Provide a captivating introduction and outline the structure of the session and your key themes. Speak with confidence and authority. Smile and pace your delivery (not too fast, not too slow).

Tell them

Develop the key themes through a cohesive narrative: a story that the interviewing panel can follow. Focus on key concepts and points.

Tell them what you have told them

Include a memorable conclusion and summarize the key points. Ask if anyone on the panel has any questions.

Good presentations require practice. Stand in front of the mirror and time yourself several times ahead of your interview. Take deep breaths and believe in yourself. Remember, the panel invited you to the interview because they believe you have the right skills, knowledge and experience for the role.

Other selection tests

There are many other available selection tests. I give a few more examples below.

Emotional intelligence tests

Someone's ability to perform a job falls is defined by three key areas: their technical skills (the skills required to undertake the role, such as employment law), their intellectual capability (commonly known as IQ) and their emotional intelligence (referred to as EI). Emotional intelligence refers to our ability to recognize, understand and manage emotions, both in ourselves and in others. Emotional intelligence is divided into four key areas: self-awareness, self-management, social awareness and relationship management. Daniel Goleman's bestselling 1995 book *Emotional Intelligence* highlights that EI contributes to 80%–90% of the competencies that distinguish outstanding leaders from average leaders.

Sample questions might include forcing you to make a choice between two statements in a pair. The key is to be spontaneous and to choose the statement that most effectively applies to you generally. An estimate of the approximate time it should take to complete the test will most likely be included. Here are some examples:

I generally learn most

- ... by actively undertaking tasks.
- ... from reflecting on past experiences.

Group differences are always

- ... causing difficulties and conflict.
- ... understood and valued.

I generally have a

- ... stronger focus on tasks rather than relationships.
- ... balanced focus on tasks and relationships.

Work sampling

Candidates might be required to complete a task or a series of tasks similar to those performed in the applied-for role. As limited time is available, only a small selection of tasks will be reviewed. Work sampling is always directly relevant to the role under review. Tasks might include payroll calculations, policy reviews or scenarios. When recruiting for people advisors and managers,

I have included a number of employment-law-related queries that are commonly asked by both managers and staff. Tasks might include the following.

Mary

Mary has just advised her manager that she is pregnant and she would like some advice regarding her entitlement to maternity leave and pay. Mary's manager, Rhianna, phones you for guidance. In no more than 500 words, please advise.

Thimmais

Thimmais requests a meeting with you regarding his workload. During the meeting he explains that workload allocation is unfair in his department and that he feels that he is being unfairly treated because he is new. He explains that he has approached his manager but nothing has changed. He is feeling overwhelmed at the moment and this is impacting his health. In no more than 500 words, please advise.

Work sampling tests are likely to be timed so do plan your time carefully. The interview team will be exploring your time management skills as well as your technical expertise.

Group discussion

Group discussion will most likely be used alongside other recruiting tests and is most often found when resourcing for graduate-level roles. The recruiting team will be assessing how you work with others, with particular emphasis on your team-working, communicating, persuading and influencing skills, as well as your ability to see different perspectives. Some of these tests might be undertaken in an assessment centre, which we discuss next.

The most effective way to manage a group discussion test is to remember that it is not about you, it is about the scenario, the team and, quite often, the ability of the group to reach agreement on a particular topic. Keeping to time is important, as is ensuring that you contribute and recognize where you might involve others. Make eye contact and listen while other group members are talking — smiling helps! It is important to be respectful, so avoid being forceful or talking over anybody.

ASSESSMENT CENTRES

During my career I have attended assessment centres as a candidate and also facilitated them in support of the hiring process. An assessment centre is a combination of tasks and activities that test your suitability for the job. The assessment centre may take place over the course of a half-day or over a couple of days. They are used in graduate recruitment and in situations where an organization is hiring for a senior position or multiple roles of the same grade, e.g. a new sales team or multiple recruitment consultants.

Assessment centres are expensive to run and time-consuming to organize, but for the hiring team they provide a good indicator of whether candidates are suitable for the post. The tests are likely to include group exercises, in-tray exercises, role plays, case studies, psychometric personality questionnaires, psychometric ability tests and competency-based interviews. Each assessment exercise is scored against a checklist. For interviewees, though, assessment centres can be uncomfortable experiences, so planning is key.

Planning for an assessment centre

Read the invitation carefully so that you know what to expect. Note what you are asked to do in preparation for the assessment centre, such as a presentation: what topic are you required to present on and for how long? Time your presentation delivery prior to the assessment day. Note what you are asked to bring with you, such as a laptop. Read through the application form/CV that you sent in response to the job advertisement. Be prepared to talk through any aspect of what you have written. What competencies are being sought for the role and what examples do you have in support of each competency?

Practise aptitude tests online if you can. Find out which test supplier the employer uses (this should be indicated in your invitation – if not, contact the people department). Find out a little about the person who will be interviewing you. How long will the interview last and what format will be used (formal, with in-depth questions, or more informal)? Use the STAR/CAR responses structures as detailed above. In group exercises remember to support and encourage other candidates and to treat everyone with courtesy and respect (see the group discussion section above).

Do not forget to plan your journey in advance so that you are familiar with the route; this will help to reduce any stress before the event. Be kind to yourself: get enough sleep prior to the event and consider your diet and exercise plan in the weeks prior to your participation. Ensure that you are at your peak and ready to tackle challenging situations!

DIFFERENT ORGANIZATIONAL APPROACHES

The number of interviews you will be required to attend for each role will depend on the organization and their resourcing policy. In some cases a decision will be made after the first interview and in others you may be required to attend two or more interviews. Some organizations may ask you to undertake a test or give a presentation, followed by competency-based, in-depth questions. Others may be far more informal. The structure and form of the interview is influenced by the culture of the organization, including its size, sector and country context. Candidates can gain useful insights about an organization through the interview process.

INTERVIEW TECHNIQUES

You have prepared responses to interview questions, you have researched the interview panel, you are dressed appropriately and you have arrived at the venue in good time (ideally 10 minutes before the start of the interview). What now?

Try to keep calm. Carry out breathing exercises if they help. It is perfectly natural to be nervous.

Breathing exercise

Let your breath flow in, as deep as possible into your stomach.
Breathe in from your nose and out through your mouth.
Breathe in gently and regularly, steadily counting 1, 2, 3, 4, 5.
Breathe out (avoid holding your breath or pausing), again counting 1, 2, 3, 4, 5.
Repeat for 3–5 minutes.

It is important to create a good first impression. Introductions will be guided by the interviewer: a hiring manager will probably introduce themselves and offer their hand to shake, for example. This will vary according to country context and culture and whether the interview is held face-to-face or online.

Wait until you are invited to sit down or until the interviewers are seated before seating yourself. Look interested and maintain good eye contact. Avoid slouching: sit upright but comfortably.

Although as a candidate you should be doing 80% of the talking, do listen when the panel are talking and indicate that you are listening by nodding and making listening noises.

When responding to questions make sure you look at the interviewer, not at the floor. Speak clearly and not too quickly (we sometimes rush when we are nervous). Avoid using jargon and really think through your response so that it is sufficiently detailed, but stop once you have responded rather than continuing to add irrelevant information.

Be as open as possible about yourself – the interviewers are trying to get to know you. Some questions might be more challenging and this might be intentional: to test your degree of interest and your skills and knowledge in relation to the post.

Some things to avoid:

- focussing on your weaknesses (emphasize your strong points and how these relate to the job);
- arguing with the interviewing panel;
- criticizing present or past employers;
- yes/no answers (provide sufficient detail so that the panel are convinced that you are the right person for the role).

When things go wrong

Despite all your good intentions, things do not always go to plan.

Case study

Jezz was on her way to an interview for a dream role as head of learning and development for a large multinational organization. The interview was scheduled to be held in London but the role itself would involve international travel. London is 70 miles on the train from Jezz's home and then she would need to catch the Tube for three stops. She had timed the journey on a practice run the week prior to her interview. Halfway into the journey the train started slowing down, and then got slower and slower. The conductor announced that the vehicle had a fault and that all passengers should disembark at the next station and wait for an alternative train. A subseqeuent announcement pronounced that the next scheduled train had been cancelled.

Jezz had no choice but to call the organization to let them know that she would not be able to make the interview on time. Luckily, the hiring manager rescheduled the interview for the following day. It is always worth communicating with the organization to keep them updated.

Case study

Talef arrived promptly for his interview, which had been arranged on his behalf by an agency. He was keen to develop his career as a people business partner and this organization – a large council in the UK – would provide a great next step, enabling Talef to develop his public sector experience. Talef was finding the questions really difficult to answer as they were tailored to compensation and reward. Although Talef had a broad overview of this area he was by no means an expert. Talef commented to the interviewers that the questions seemed very specific and targeted at reward whereas Talef was more of a generalist and was looking to focus on all aspects of the people profession as a business partner. The interviewers looked a little surprised and clarified that the vacancy was for a compensation and reward specialist. After further discussion they found that the recruitment agency had sent Talef to the wrong interview! It is always a good idea to check the job role at the beginning of the interview.

Case study

It makes sense to dress appropriately for an interview: to ensure that your shoes are clean and that your suit or dress is ironed if required. Monica had planned her outfit in advance, diligently prepared for the interview and was 5 minutes away from the venue when a child ran into her, spilling a bottle of Coca-Cola over her outfit. She was soaking wet and started to panic. Luckily, she was in the centre of a city, surrounded by shops. She found a dress in the sale at the front of a store, asked to try it on, kept it on, paid and ran to the interview. Although not as calm as she had been, she was only marginally late and looked smart in her new outfit – which was only slightly too big for her.

SUMMARY

Much of this chapter is dedicated to preparatory work: researching the company, the role, the panel and the likely interview questions prior to the interview. This is because success at the interview stage requires considerable homework prior to the event. Being organized can significantly reduce stress and anxiety levels on the day. A variety of selection tests may be included as part of the interview process, including psychometric tests, motivation questionnaires, critical reasoning tests, emotional intelligence exercises, simulation tests, presentation skills, in-tray exercises and work sampling. Hiring managers may select one or two tests to help them determine the best candidate for the role. Some organizations favour assessment centres, particularly when hiring graduates or resourcing for multiple roles. Assessment centres are likely to include multiple tests and a competency-based interview. Whatever form your interview takes and whichever tests you are required to complete, remember that preparation is the key to success!

Chapter 9

THE FUTURE OF HR

IN CHAPTER 1 WE EXPLORED the evolution of people management and the speed at which roles have developed, from welfare officer to strategic business partner. In this chapter we consider the future of work and how the people management roles that we are familiar with today will need to evolve.

We are currently living through the fourth industrial revolution – or, as some people refer to it, industry 4.0. Industrial innovations include electricity, assembly lines, computerization and now cyber-physical systems, with smart technologies enabling connected machines to interact with each other and even make decisions autonomously. Advances in technology and the global business landscape, changing demographic trends, greater competition and shifting customer needs are impacting how organizations operate. This fourth industrial revolution is set to disrupt every aspect of our lives, offering opportunities for us to improve our quality of life, raise our income levels, become more efficient and enhance the way we plan. But it is also possible that we will see further segregation in the job market, where lower-level skills will be poorly rewarded and higher-level skills will be attractively remunerated. Some jobs will become obsolete, and the speed of change might be such that organizations find it difficult to keep up. These structural shifts are impacting both the supply of and the demand for talent.

This chapter is divided into three sections: 'Digital landscape', 'People philosophy' and 'Organization design'. The ordering should not be considered a carefully calibrated, prioritized list, but it does focus on the three key aspects of change that people professionals will likely need to focus on in the future.

DIGITAL LANDSCAPE

To take advantage of the opportunities ahead, people and organizations need to be proactive in harnessing technology that can reshape the reality we take for granted today. Technology is now available that can completely transform the people management landscape. But just talking about the potential of digital transformation in organizations is of little help in actually driving change; instead, we need to focus on practical application. For example, technology has already transformed recruiting tools in some businesses, automating the time-consuming recruitment process and enabling people professionals to effectively manage the increasing amount of data associated with resourcing talent.

Artificial intelligence

Artificial intelligence, or AI, refers to the ability of a computer or machine to simulate the human mind. The computer learns from examples and experience and is capable of making decisions and solving problems. This can be particularly helpful at the start of the recruitment process when sourcing, screening and nurturing candidates. Not only does it save time and money, it also helps to tackle human bias and delivers effective candidate matches. However, like any system it is only as good as the algorithms built into it: algorithms that are tainted with bias and assumptions will impact on the application results.

Case study

IBM uses AI to screen output such as work samples, social media posts, facial expressions and speech patterns to detect signs of bigotry, violence, curiosity, and so on, in order to find employees that are the best fit for the culture of the organization.[31] AI offers the potential for creating a more diverse workforce that can improve the whole employee experience through the sourcing of employees who will creative an inclusive culture, where everyone belongs.

Chatbots (or conversational user interfaces) can also support people processes and are used extensively in the recruitment process to gather initial candidate requirements, provide preliminary screening, book interviews and respond to candidate questions. Chatbots are increasingly being used to support employee self-service portals, providing staff with quick responses to questions such as 'How much holiday entitlement do I have left?' and enabling staff to update their own personal details such as a change of address.

Case study

IKEA switched to an electronic application process in Eastern Europe and subsequently found a steep decline in applications.[32] This was due to the lengthy, tedious process that required candidates to create accounts before they were able to apply for an open position. Using chatbots simplified the process, making it easier and more interactive. The chatbot was able to see which qualifications were required for each job position, so it could show candidates which positions they were qualified for. Streamlining the process enabled people professionals to capture candidate data efficiently, thus supporting the sourcing of candidates.

Virtual reality

Virtual reality is a simulated experience that can be similar to or completely different from the world we live in. It is a three-dimensional, computer-generated environment that we can explore and interact with. In the practical sense, it provides opportunities for recruiting, onboarding and training. In recruitment, virtual reality might be used in simulations to test candidate skills. It can also be used in onboarding, where companies can use virtual reality to recreate training environments that are less dangerous than the real workplace – a construction site, for example. Here, virtual reality can be used to teach both health and safety and good practice. Virtual reality has transformed the training landscape, providing opportunities for employees to easily experience different environments and cultures, e.g. cross-cultural training.

Data analytics

Data analytics involves applying an algorithmic or mechanical process to determine insights from several data sets in order to arrive at meaningful conclusions. People analytics is the use of people data in analytical processes to solve business issues. People professionals hold a considerable amount of data, including candidate applications, employee profiles, payroll records and performance records. Analytics allows people professionals to make data-driven decisions rather than relying on gut reactions.

Although people management departments have been keeping records for many years, there is now a need to turn these data into information and insight. Analytics allows people managers to contribute to decision making at a strategic level. To be effective, data from different systems must be combined in order to assess impact. For example, if we want to explore the effect of employee engagement on financial performance, annual engagement survey results need to be analysed in relation to financial performance data. Analytics provides an opportunity to look at the traits of the workforce and the value of the skills and experience both of individuals and of teams (known as human capital), so that people professionals are able to demonstrate the impact of people processes and policies on workforce and organizational development.

People management ecosystems are evolving, with an increasing focus on the use of cloud-based technology rather than on-premises software to support payroll, workforce management, talent management, and so on. Additionally, despite the potential for all-in-one platforms to support every area of the people management function, ensuring a holistic and seamless approach, this is not viable for every organization, and it remains difficult for companies to achieve complete functionality from a single people management system. According to a 2019 white paper, the average number of individual applications used across businesses of all sizes was 7.53.[33] The focus now is on creating a method whereby these different applications can communicate with each other, so that the various individual functions perform more effectively than an all-in-one platform.

Risk and privacy

Organizations are increasingly building and using integrated systems to analyse worker-related data. This provides the ability to monitor people data from many sources, including social media and survey data from integrated people management systems. According to *Deloitte Insights Magazine*, advanced analytics can track and analyse voice communications, personal interactions, video interviews and even the sentiment of employee emails.[34] Software is now available that can interpret email traffic to monitor employee stress levels and to stop fraud and poor management. Although analytics presents huge opportunities, it also presents significant risks. Europe's General Data Protection Regulation (GDPR) defines high-risk data as data which are 'likely to result in high risk for the rights and freedoms of individuals', and data thus identified require greater protection.[35] Companies require robust policies, security, transparency and open communication to mitigate the risks associated with people data and analytics, which could otherwise ultimately impact their employer brand in terms of financial and legal liability, not to mention the harm that could be done to employees themselves.

As discussed above, algorithms and machine-based decisions are only as good as the data they are programmed with. Also, AI requires people to monitor social networking and advertising algorithms to ensure that the data make sense and are being interpreted effectively. Moreover, cybersecurity is a key priority for business today, and the risk of attack is expected to become ever greater for businesses in the future. People professionals play a critical role in managing risk, through training and educating colleagues, conducting proper risk assessments, communicating the company's responsibilities and ensuring that good data security is at the centre of all processes and practices.

PEOPLE PHILOSOPHY

Individualization

Traditional views of people management tend to focus on the workforce as a functional team or organization with a common goal. Collectivism promotes the benefits of the collective and encourages members to adopt a group's values, ideas and beliefs. However, the degree of specialization and the variety of motivations and preferences of the contemporary workforce require organizations to consider the individual needs of their staff. Providing a culture where individuals can celebrate their own rights and beliefs allows them to come up with their own way of doing the job. It can encourage and enhance creativity, collaboration and high levels of performance. Individualization is linked to the reduction in the practical role of trade unions in establishing the content of employment contracts in comparison with an increase in individual agreements. Ultimately, employees want choice and will need different things from their work, their line manager and their career at various times. This means people professionals will need to consider the person rather than the worker, and they will need to ensure that policies can be adapted to suit the needs of the individual in different circumstances.

The changing workforce

Workforce demographics have changed considerably over the decades. The 2017 UK Department for Work and Pensions report 'Fuller working lives' showed that the number of people aged 50 or over within the workforce had grown to 9.8 million by 2016 – that is 2.2 million more than in 2006 and 4.1 million more than two decades ago.[36] According to a June 2020 Office for National Statistics report, many more women are working than was the case 50 years ago: 72.7% of women aged 16–64 are employed now, compared with 52.8% in 1971.[37] In comparison, 80.1% of men aged 16–64 are currently employed. Statistics additionally identify five generations – see below – that are currently part of today's workforce.[38]

- Traditionalists/the silent generation (born 1925–1945) are considered to be loyal conformists. They value job title and money.
- Baby boomers (born 1946–1964) are deemed to be loyal, work-centric and cynical. They value job titles and both monetary and non-monetary rewards, e.g. flexible retirement planning.
- Generation X members (born 1965–1980) are seen as independent workers who require minimal supervision. They value flexible schedules, promotions based on competence and opportunities to grow.

- Generation Y/millennials (born 1981–1994) are described as tech-savvy. They prefer to work for the highest bidder and as a result they are likely to jump from one organization to another. They value flexible schedules, the right working environment and embracing the latest technology.
- Generation Z/alpha members (born after the mid 1990s) are judged to be highly tech-savvy (having received their first mobile phone at an average age of 10). They have grown up in a hyper-connected world and the smartphone is their preferred mode of communication. They seek workplace flexibility and highly collaborative management relationships.

The range of generations in employment presents a number of challenges for people professionals. Certainly, it seems that traditional notions of hierarchy and seniority will not fit well with the expectations of generations Y and Z. There is an ever-increasing desire for flexible working arrangements, and the Covid-19 pandemic – which has resulted in many organizations enforcing home working– has accentuated this desire. Employees are therefore increasingly likely to demand better well-being options, so organizations and people professionals will need to consider how they can increase resilience in order to sustain well-being.

Case study

The DIY retailer B&Q has designed its recruitment strategy to attract a diverse age range, with a specific focus on older generations.[39] The company acknowledges and appreciates that age brings a wealth of skills and experience. An employee benefits case study in 2011 found that 28% of B&Q's workforce was over the age of 50, with the eldest employee, who worked on their checkouts, being 96. The case study noted that adjustments were in place to support people with injuries, those becoming more frail with age and so on, and this enabled workers from older generations to continue working. This approach is part of a differentiated well-being strategy and is likely to increase in the future.

Workers aged 65 and over will constitute more than half of all UK employment growth over the next decade – accounting for 282,000 new employees out of a total of 546,000 – according to 2019 data from the Office for National Statistics.[40] Some people might choose to continue working in a job they love, while others might find part-time work that allows them to top up their pension pot; others might need to work for financial reasons. Whatever the motivation, UK population projections indicate large increases in the over-65s in the decades to come, and organizations must ensure that well-being strategies reflect the needs of this diverse workforce.

While generalizations regarding generational discussions are helpful for emphasizing key characteristics of changing demographics, assumptions do need to be considered with care. These descriptions make sweeping statements about large groups of the population, contradicting the growing recognition of individualism in discussions. For example, a twenty-something may well be seeking the same flexible benefits package and well-being support as someone in the sixty-five plus bracket. People professionals must ensure that policies are tailored to the needs of individuals regardless of generational descriptions and age.

Employee experience

It has long been recognized that happy employees are more productive – precisely 13% happier according to research undertaken by the Oxford University Said Business School and BT in 2019, which found a conclusive link between these factors in their report 'Does employee happiness have an impact on productivity?'[41] Employees increasingly demand an engaging, productive and enjoyable work experience and yet organizations have traditionally measured worker satisfaction once a year through a staff survey. More recently, employers have focused on how to engage employees to ensure that they give their best to the organization. Employee engagement is about creating a workplace that provides the right conditions for all staff to be able to perform effectively every day, with a commitment to their organization's goals, mission, vision and values, in order to contribute to the organization's success.

Employee experience focuses on all aspects of the employee lifecycle: it is how an employee sees, hears and feels about their employment, from recruitment to employee exit. Candidates assess future employers from the very start of the talent acquisition process in terms of values, well-being, technology, reward and recognition, the physical environment, leadership, development, teams, products and services. Employee experience is therefore about the day-to-day lived experience of employees, and this must be positively affected to achieve employee engagement. While employee *engagement* might be viewed as a top-down initiative that focuses on culture, purpose and work, employee *experience* is a bottom-up approach that considers how the employee perceives each stage of their employee journey. Failure to consider the employee experience can severely impact the employer brand, as in the following case.

Case study

The net worth of Amazon's CEO Jeff Bezos is approximately US$100 billion, yet Amazon warehouse workers have been reported to work for long hours in difficult conditions under close supervision, being given only 9 seconds to process packages. Stories like this have a damaging impact on an employer's brand.

The employee experience is set to be one of the key priorities for people professionals in the future. Employee expectations are increasing, so if organizations are to attract the best talent they will need to adopt a more employee-centric mindset, putting employees first and ensuring that they are at the heart of every decision. Organizations now need to align the experience of their internal customers (employees) with their external customers (consumers). Many companies recognize the value of the customer experience as a key element of their business culture and brand, and they also realize the extent to which this supports differentiation in the marketplace. A 2012 study titled 'Employee satisfaction and engagement once again linked to financial success', out of Northwestern University in the US, found that there are direct links between employee satisfaction and customer satisfaction and between customer satisfaction and improved financial performance. More recently, the correlation was further established in a 2017 MIT study, cited in the Deloitte Insights 2019 Global Human Capital Trends report, which found that companies that provide a great employee experience are 25% more profitable than those that do not. People professionals will need to work closely with other parts of their business to align employee and customer experience strategies.

Talent management

The Global Talent 2021 report from Oxford Economics found that employers are demanding new skills from their employees and yet they find that these are in short supply. This is in spite of the fact that, according to the International Labour Organization, 40 million workers in the industrialized world were unemployed in 2019.[42] In fact, 41% of executives rated 'competing for talent globally' as one of their most pressing talent concerns. In response, more talent is being home grown, and it is forecast that in some parts of the world a surplus of talent will be generated. In the US and much of Europe, critical reskilling is taking place in response to the demands of a highly digitized and interconnected world, where higher-level skills are required. People professionals will increasingly be required to develop more evidence-based approaches to managing talent by using analytics to determine skills gaps and to optimize the allocation of talent in response to workforce plans. Developing a workforce with the digital skills, resilience and agility to survive today's challenges while also driving competitive advantage in the future requires organizations to commit to upskilling their workforces. The 23rd Annual Global CEO Survey undertaken by PWC in 2020 found that 74% of CEOs were concerned about the availability of key skills.[43] What skills might be required in the future is a moving target, certainly, but people need to learn how to think, act and thrive in an unpredictable digital world. In order to survive, organizations will need to adapt to situations in an agile way.

Performance management

Traditional performance management systems have long been recognized as being ineffective, and they are disliked by managers for being time-consuming and by employees for being overly subjective, unhelpful and ultimately demotivating. Organizations are slowly starting to do something about it, moving away from the annual evaluation ritual and towards methods that promote continual feedback and coaching. Companies are now starting to focus more on individuals who are at either the lower or the higher end of the performance spectrum, using objective performance systems that allow a more fact-based discussion to take place when needed and at more frequent intervals.

Case study

Netflix has overhauled their performance management process by moving away from annual performance evaluations and towards regular, more informal reviews.[44] In their new programme, employees were advised what they should stop, start or continue to do. Feedback was provided anonymously to start with, but the organization has now developed 360-degree reviews. Netflix advocated transparency and truth in their feedback process.

People professionals will be instrumental to the changes required to enhance employee feedback mechanisms in their organizations, moving away from traditional annual reviews and towards processes that develop a continuous feedback loop. Training managers to be coaches who engage in frequent, specific feedback to support future-focused development will be key to increasing the impact of feedback discussions.

The global talent landscape and the extended workforce

One of the biggest challenges for organizations of all sizes, whether operating globally or nationally, is building and sustaining a strong talent pipeline to ensure they remain competitive. A knowledge-based economy relies on a highly qualified labour force in all sectors of the economy and society. This involves resourcing talent internally through succession pools and promotions to ensure self-sustainable pools for future leaders, and also resourcing externally through the competition for talent. Workforces need to learn, adapt and grow in the face of constant disruption and fast-paced change.

Talent attraction needs to be integrated into the overall business strategy. People professionals need to consider the overall company goals and develop strategic relationships with managers to align priorities and strategies. Both an internal strategy and an external one will be required, and the employer brand is an integral part of both. Moreover, the workforce will increasingly transcend geographical boundaries because staff are working remotely in different country contexts. People professionals will be crucial in supporting managers to communicate with, support and manage an increasingly diverse workforce.

Although some organizations have made progress in their promotion of diversity and inclusion, there is still considerable work to be done in addressing structural inclusion. To date, work in this area has focused on addressing unconscious bias, but more work is needed to explore how both conscious and unconscious bias have filtered through to organizations' people management systems and processes in pay and rewards, promotions, development, resourcing decisions, and so on. People professionals will need to work with senior leaders to address inherent biases in organizational systems.

Working in a multicultural environment can be an enriching experience that promotes awareness and understanding of different viewpoints and expertise. This in turn supports problem-solving, stimulates creativity and potentially increases profits. A 2018 study of 1,000 companies across twelve countries by McKinsey & Company found that companies in the top quartile for gender diversity were 21% more likely to experience above-average profitability, while ethnic and cultural diversity resulted in a 33% increase in performance.[45] Diversity is celebrated by Apple, as demonstrated by the case study below.

Case study

Apple describes itself as 'different together'.[46]

'At Apple, we're not the same. And that's our greatest strength. We draw on the differences in who we are, what we've experienced, and how we think. Because to create products that serve everyone, we believe in including everyone.'

There are also a growing number of people who temporarily lend companies their skills and knowledge in an ever-expanding network of freelancers, consultants and outsourcing partners. Economists predict that this trend is set to increase. Many of these workers are highly skilled, top performers, and increasingly they are mobile, borderless and global. Using collaborative tools and technology can support the workforce to interact effectively together and build a sense of community, gain access to resources for completing work and aid social contact. People professionals will be able to leverage technology to apply performance feedback, learning and knowledge management to the extended workforce.

Democratization of the workplace

Workplace democracy is the application of democracy in the workplace through principles such as voting, debate and participatory decision making. With the rapid advances in technology, agile working environments and an emphasis on the employee experience, workplace democracy is likely to become increasingly promoted by organizations. It makes good business sense to engage staff and allow them an opportunity to voice their ideas and experiences. Inviting participation and involvement from people within the organization will lead to a more integrated organization, allowing for more efficient problem-solving and higher levels of commitment. It can also help build team relationships and increase morale and job satisfaction. But to achieve this, organizations may need to make some fundamental changes to their culture to facilitate this type of working. Companies will need to be transparent by sharing critical and new information with teams and individuals, and by sharing feedback. Hierarchies should be avoided so that all departments are treated equally and fairly, and responsibility should be delegated.

ORGANIZATION DESIGN

Agile organizations

The McKinsey & Company Insights report in 2018 reveals five hallmarks of agile organizations, highlighting flexible resource allocation, sensing and seizing opportunities, clear flat structures, rapid iteration and experimentation and next-generation enabling technology as key features.[47] Essentially, an agile organization is focused on customer needs, so it is quick to respond to changes in the marketplace or environment.

As more organizations respond to the need for agility and recognize its benefits, shifts in management style and work culture may well be required. People professionals will need to work with the senior team to ensure that their organization's vision and values are aligned with its purpose. The most successful transformations happen from the bottom up, and managers must communicate with their teams to enable rather than control their work. In order to make fast progress, people professionals might consider creating learning flows that align with work flows, so that training and development takes place when and how required, in a purposeful way. Checking how people are feeling through regular pulse surveys provides timely updates and enables changes to be made when required. Ensuring that people stay connected through virtual collaboration will be important.

Case study

The Boston Consulting Group in New York designed an office space that created the opportunity for unplanned collisions in order to transform their office culture.[48] Increasingly, people will need a compelling reason to go to work: to make connections, to learn and to innovate. The new office design emphasized fluidity through the use of specialist spaces that allowed effective sharing of the workspace. Portable technology that was untethered from the desk supported workforce agility.

Since the Covid-19 pandemic, organizations have recognized the benefits of agile, flexible and home working. This has led to a growing debate on the future of the workspace. It seems increasingly likely that few people will return to the exact work regime they had in early 2020. Organizations that were already considering their use of space are now planning more agile working patterns going forward. For people professionals, agile working can be a cultural challenge. Managing people effectively in an agile organization requires teams and individuals to adopt different working practices – something that will challenge existing taken-for-granted processes across the organization.

The hybrid organization

Numerous studies carried out during the pandemic suggest that despite people's struggles with home working during the preliminary stages of lockdown, there is now an increasing appetite for a permanent change to remote working. *Forbes* reported that a study carried out by Creative Strategies in February 2021 found that 46% of respondents expressed a desire to work from home as often as possible, with a further 31% saying they would like to work from home a couple of days a week.[49] Only 17% were keen to get back to the office. Hybrid models of work allow for some staff to work at home while others work on site.

Google surveyed their people about working preferences in 2020 and found that most were keen to get back to the office – but not full time.[50] The company intends to develop a full hybrid model of working that they believe will result in greater productivity, collaboration and well-being: goals that are at the centre of Google's workplace philosophy. The German multinational company Siemens AG plans to move to a new permanent mobile-working scheme where its 140,000 employees can work from home two or three days a week.[51] The CIPD conducted research in 2020 and found that employers expect the proportion of people working from home on a regular basis to increase from 18% to 37%, with 22% of staff working from home all the time compared with just 9% before the pandemic.[52]

The hybrid organization presents considerable advantages because, by diminishing geographical boundaries, it enables employers to recruit from a much wider pool of talent. Such flexibility will also ensure that work is more accessible and sustainable, which provides a better work–life balance, supporting those with caring responsibilities or concerns over mobility or health. Organizations will benefit from a more diverse workforce, which will in turn encourage innovation and improve cultural insights, resulting in a wider range of skills and ultimately improving productivity. The key challenge for people professionals will be to ensure that all aspects of the employee lifecycle are capable of supporting the hybrid workforce in order to promote a sense of belonging and collegiality among employees. A culture should be designed to make location irrelevant while maximizing opportunities for ongoing collaboration.

Organizational purpose and culture

The Covid-19 pandemic has brought about a seismic shift in how traditional lines of communication and reporting are structured and delivered. Organizations that were previously concerned about remote working for fear that productivity would drop have found the reverse to be true, as more employers have learned to trust their staff to get on with their jobs.

Companies have spent a great deal of time and money on demonstrating their purpose and authenticity in recent years, and the pandemic has placed this in the spotlight as people are reminded of their own mortality. For people professionals this provides an opportunity to help shape a workforce that has different drivers, purposes and ways of working. Deloitte's 2016 survey 'Transitioning to the future of work and the workplace' (which was sponsored by Facebook) found that 69% of those surveyed believed that company culture, especially transparency in communication, is critically important if an organization is to achieve its vision and mission.[53] Cultures will need to change in many organizations to support different decision-making structures and new ways of communicating. We are likely to see a movement from top-down to collaborative leadership, emphasizing a facilitating and coaching approach that is nurturing and supportive.

The CIPD note in their research into the people profession of 2030 that in addition to the technological and digital transformation, changing demographics and the diversity and inclusion strategies noted above, sustainability and responsible business are key aspects of the workplace going forward.[54] People professionals will need to champion a strategic approach to responsible business, weaving social value and purpose through the entire employee lifecycle by ensuring that each aspect of the people function reflects a widening remit on corporate social responsibility and organizational purpose and values.

WHAT DOES ALL THIS MEAN FOR YOUR CAREER IN THE PEOPLE PROFESSION?

The world of work is changing rapidly. One of the most significant areas for people professionals will be the extent to which we will all need to become increasingly 'tech savvy' in order to make an impact and to add value to an organization. The importance of people analytics and the ability to apply analytical and predictive techniques to enhance resourcing strategies and predict performance are essential skills to ensure that people professionals equip themselves to be suitably future-focused. HR processes are likely to become increasingly automated and streamlined, and people professionals will need to facilitate this so that they are prepared to take advantage of the improved efficiency and insights that new systems are able to provide. Being able to collect data is one thing, but having the skills to analyse and communicate those data is critically important to ensuring an impactful contribution to organizations. Although people professionals can attend training, there will be an increasing focus on self-learning in order to build effective capability to contribute to business change.

Being able to lead in a digital world, to manage digital transformation and change, and to ensure that one's workforce is appropriately prepared for the changes that lie ahead will require people professionals that understand the strategic direction of their organization, the economic and social environment in which their company operates, and ultimately how to build a workforce where employees are happy and productive and where they are developed appropriately to maximize their ability to contribute. People professionals will need to have strong knowledge in diversity and inclusion and they will need to be aware that policies and processes must be tailored to the needs of a multigenerational workforce. This enables people professionals to be effective project managers and, crucially, to be able to communicate with everyone, both digitally and in person.

SUMMARY

Both work and the workplace are set to change considerably over the coming decades. This presents people professionals with a considerable opportunity to influence working practices and to enable organizations to flourish. Advances in technology and data analytics will provide tools that people professionals can use to add value like never before, giving evidence to support strategic decisions and influence change. Technology will increasingly reduce the transactional nature of the people function so that more time can be spent ensuring that the organization is prepared for the complex, ambiguous and dynamic work landscape.

The agile and hybrid workplace of the future will require new skills that facilitate a collaborative space, where leaders and managers become 'alongsiders', coaching and enabling employees, to aid high-performance working. People professionals will increasingly be working globally to attract and retain talent and manage a multigenerational and diverse workforce. At the same time, policies will become progressively individualized, tailored to the needs of employees with flexibility and well-being at the centre of the employee experience. People professionals will need to work closely with the senior team to ensure resilient leaders are in place to manage a distributed workforce.

Chapter 10

CONTINUING PROFESSIONAL DEVELOPMENT AND CAREER PROGRESSION

IN THIS FINAL CHAPTER WE explore continuing professional development (CPD) and how this supports career progress. We discuss the various ways in which CPD can be undertaken and we reflect on activities that will inform the compilation of a plan to support career advancement. A number of tools to support career development are introduced along with examples of how they might be used. CPD templates are included and discussed. The last section of the chapter focuses on 'looking ahead to stay ahead', helping you ensure that your skills and knowledge are continually updated and helping you to plan not just your next career move but ultimately how to achieve your dream role.

Many people spend more time planning their vacation than their career. But why leave things to chance? After all, work is one of the most time-intensive elements of our life (many people spend 40 or 50 years of their lives working). CPD is about putting ourselves in control so that our career is less a series of random events and more a proactive plan in support of our future career aspirations. It is about stretching ourselves so that we reach a successful and fulfilling career.

WHAT IS CONTINUING PROFESSIONAL DEVELOPMENT?

CPD is a way to reflect on what we have achieved and to take action in support of our aspirations. It is an ongoing process that puts each of us in the driving seat so that we are in control of our learning and development journey. The CIPD defines CPD as follows:

> CPD is a combination of approaches, ideas and techniques that will help you manage your own learning and growth. The focus of CPD is firmly on results – the benefits that professional development can bring you in the real world.[55]

CPD is very individual – what is right for me may not suit you – and it therefore requires each of us to really reflect on what we have done and what we hope to achieve in the future. This provides us with purpose and direction. We must take responsibility for managing our own learning goals, setting our own targets and integrating learning into our work activities.

Undertaking and managing CPD provides you with a structured approach to managing your career. It provides evidence that you are committed to your own development and offers you a framework in which you can keep track of your performance. CPD enables you to assess the areas in which you could improve and focus on your achievements – all of which is helpful for job applications and interviews.

Sometimes when I am delivering training sessions or working with students on professional development, people tell me that their organization manages their CPD for them. They are directed to what they must learn and which goals they need to achieve. I refer to this as passive CPD, where the professional is receiving learning. Organizational goals cascade into individual development plans. Organizations guide their staff towards the skills, knowledge and behaviours that they need you to have to meet their goals. But what about *your* goals? Do these not transcend your organization?

Professional development goals are likely to be influenced by the needs of your current employer, but also by professional bodies and your individual career aspirations. Being a CPD activist puts you in control. It requires you to look inwards – assessing your strengths, weaknesses, opportunities and threats (the SWOT analysis) – as well as outwards towards your chosen professional standards, the requirements of your organization and the environment that you are working in, whether this be local, national or global. Let us start by conducting an individual SWOT analysis.

SWOT analysis

SWOT stands for strengths, weaknesses, opportunities and threats, and a SWOT analysis can help you to evaluate past, present and future individual career goals. Strengths and opportunities are areas that are favourable and within your control, while weaknesses might represent areas for development and threats can be dictated by external forces. The key is to explore the correlation between your strengths and weaknesses and how to leverage your strengths to make the most of your opportunities. You might also consider how to improve your weaknesses in order to mitigate threats.

Undertaking a SWOT analysis can be very helpful in gaining deeper insights to inform your career plan. It is not something that can be done in a hurry. Do set aside some time for reflection and revisit the analysis several times over the period of a few weeks to ensure that you capture a full picture of your current situation.

Here are some questions to consider for each of the four categories.

Strengths

- What are your positive traits?
- What are you good at?

- What are your educational achievements?
- What do other people see as your strengths?
- What resources do you have?

Weaknesses

- What tasks do you avoid?
- What resources are you lacking?
- In what areas do you require more training or education?
- What fears do you have that might be holding you back?
- What are your negative habits?

Opportunities

- How can you use your strengths to create opportunities?
- How can you turn your weaknesses into opportunities?
- Who in your network can help you?
- How is your role/sector/industry changing?
- What new technology can help you reach your goals?

Threats

- Are you competing with others for what you want?
- Is your job, health or life changing?
- Could any of your weaknesses prevent you from succeeding?
- Do you have any obligations that may limit your development?
- Do any of your strengths hold you back?

An example SWOT analysis

In table 11 on the facing page, Tanya reflects on her current position as an HR advisor in a small charity that employs eighty staff, alongside her previous work experience, skills, knowledge and competencies.

Why not try compiling your own SWOT analysis using the format above before reading on?

Table 11 An example SWOT analysis: Tanya.

Strengths	Weaknesses
Interpersonal skills and ability to build relationships at all levels High degree of self-motivation Experience of leading volunteers Strong work ethic and positive reputation in existing role.	Limited exposure to strategic context in previous work roles Limited experience in a commercial capacity as most work undertaken in third sector Tendency to focus too much on the detail without seeing the bigger picture
Opportunities	**Threats**
To undertake professional qualifications to help me stand out as a people professional To develop employee relations experience in my current role To further my people management skills in a voluntary capacity (outside my core role) to gain more experience	I have only worked in SMEs, which means I have limited enterprise exposure and this may hinder my ability to compete effectively with other candidates when applying to multinational organizations The fast pace of technological developments impacts the evolution of the people function and I have limited exposure to new systems as my current company cannot afford to invest

If you now have an idea of your core strengths, weaknesses, opportunities and threats, you may wish to tailor your professional development priorities in relation to your career aspirations or your next career move.

Perhaps you are at the very beginning of your career as a people professional. A useful starting point for a development audit is to be guided by one of the competency frameworks used by relevant professional bodies (see chapter 3). The SHRM HR competencies are usefully divided into people, organization and workplace, where you can assess your current skills, knowledge and experience against each. Similarly, the CIPD uses the HR profession map as a framework of competence that details core behaviours, core knowledge and specialist knowledge.[56] Other professional bodies that are dedicated to the people profession will include similar competency standards. Choose the one that is most relevant to you in the country/company that you are working in or would like to work in. Do remember that some professional bodies have reciprocal agreements that recognize the transferability of key people competencies.

Also note that each of the competency levels are targeted at different experience levels. Your skills audit will map onto where you are in your career journey. For example, the CIPD will explain that work at foundation level is likely to be tactical and focused on the day-to-day delivery of tasks. Practitioners will gather information to use in their role, and use information to understand their work, their organization and the profession. At foundation level practitioners will work with and deliver immediate and short-term outcomes for their manager, colleagues and customers. In comparison, at the chartered fellow level work is likely to be much more strategic, with a significant level of complexity. Practitioners will develop evidence-based thinking to shape the profession or drive people change. They will influence stakeholders and create long-term value. Therefore, be realistic: where are you now and where do you want to be?

The skills gap analysis

Conducting a skills gap analysis is a three-part process. It involves assessing your current skills, determining your desired skills and identifying any gaps. This exercise will help inform your priorities for learning and development.

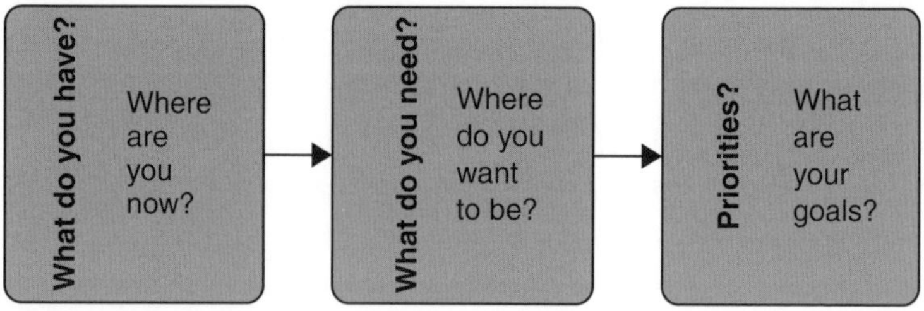

Figure 7 Skills audit.

Having undertaken the skills audit using prospective job role descriptions or competency-based frameworks, you may have a better idea of your key priorities for development areas that will enable you to secure your first role or a new one. It is a good idea to view job boards weekly so that you have a strong awareness of what employers are seeking. You may find it useful to check the following sites for roles related to people management:

- www.glassdoor.co.uk
- https://pmjobs.cipd.co.uk
- https://jobs.personneltoday.com
- www.linkedin.com/jobs
- www.seek.com.au/jobs-in-human-resources-recruitment
- www.indeed.com/jobs

Assessing your priorities

When assessing our development needs it is important to be realistic about what can be achieved in the time available. Explore what is achievable and be kind to yourself. Maslow's hierarchy of needs (see chapter 1 and figure 8, overleaf) initially highlighted five levels of human needs that allow an individual to be fulfilled.[57] The hierarchy is an influential motivation theory in psychology, and it can be usefully tailored to the workplace to help us explore our priorities at any given time. Maslow later noted how self-transcendence brings the individual 'peak experiences' that go beyond our own personal concerns and often bring a greater sense of self-fulfilment, peace and joy through our connection with others.

If you are an experienced people practitioner, you might be seeking more opportunities that will allow you to share your experiences and support those who are less experienced. In contrast, if you are at the beginning of your career, you may be seeking opportunities to learn more about the people profession through colleagues and

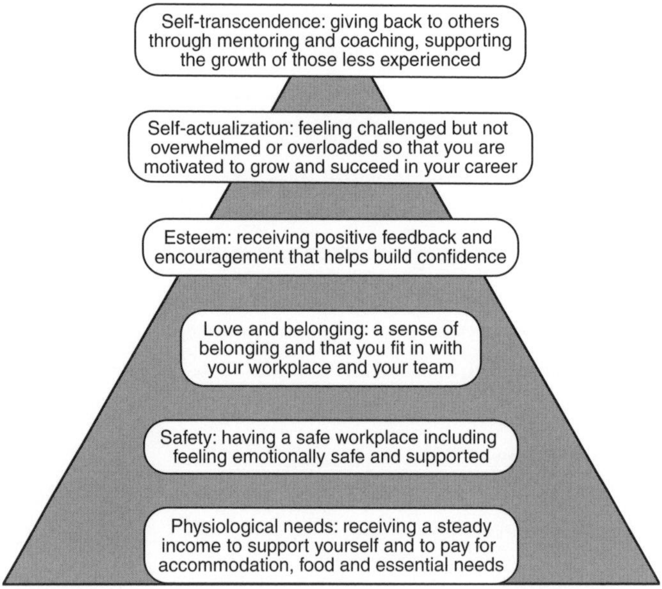

Figure 8 Maslow's hierarchy of needs adapted to the workplace.

in an environment that will provide you with opportunities to grow your knowledge and skills. Perhaps you are seeking a role where you will be supported with learning and development. You may wish to specialize in a particular area, such as compensation and reward, well-being or people analytics.

A point of reflection

What are your current priorities? And what do you need from your workplace to help you achieve them?

DEFINING SUCCESS

When we are considering our career and the roles(s) that we aspire to, it is worth taking a step back to assess what success looks like to us. How do *you* define success?

Too often we carry with us someone else's definition of success (the outside-in perspective). We take our view of success from what others deem important and we assess ourselves according to their measurement of success. More often than not, Western society equates success with achieving more. But what about you? What really matters? If we take an inside-out perspective, we might consider that success is more likely to be achieved through doing less and being more spontaneous and flexible.

Explore your own view of success by completing the following statements.

- My line manager will think that I am successful when I ...
- My family/friends will think that I am a successful when I ...
- I shall think that I am a successful when I ...
- In order to achieve this I need to ...

When we assess our priorities and use the inside-out perspective of what we deem to be most important, it is worth spending some time exploring our values.

The values audit

When you are looking at career transitions it is of course not just about what you are able to offer your future employer but also what they are able to offer you. To what extent do the values of the organization align with your own? Values really matter. Table 12 on the next page shows you what some example organizations stand for.

What are your values?

Take a look at table 13 overleaf for inspiration. Consider which ten of the values listed are most important to you. Do not be afraid to deviate from this list — it is only included as a guide.

Table 12 Organizational values.

Facebook We are bold, open and we focus on impact, move fast and build social value	**Amazon** We are customer-obsessed and we have long-term thinking, the eagerness to invest and pride in operational excellence
HSBC We value difference, we succeed together, we take responsibility and we get it done	**Teva Pharmaceuticals** We innovate where we create value, getting it done together, leading the way, caring, with focus and accountability, making our families proud

Table 13 Some possible values.

Authenticity	Determination	Leadership	Risk	Structure
Achievement	Fairness	Mastery	Realism	Tolerance
Autonomy	Fun	Meaning	Reflection	Talent
Balance	Happiness	Motivation	Significance	Toughness
Boldness	Honesty	Openness	Smartness	Vision
Compassion	Innovation	Persistence	Spontaneity	Vigour
Challenge	Impact	Power	Simplicity	Vitality
Creativity	Kindness	Professionalism	Security	Unity

Also consider values based on family, integrity, achievement, feelings and freedom. What is important to you and what is *most* important to you? Try to prioritize your top ten values. Reflect on your list and revisit it again after a few days. Does it represent your priorities? Once you are clear about your values, you are in a stronger position to identify organizations that effectively align with what you consider to be most important.

So far we have explored our skills, knowledge and experience through a SWOT analysis for generic insights, and then through more specific competency models and job role descriptions to gain a more precise representation for our professional development audit. We have also started to explore our definition of success and our priority values. These reflections will be helpful in informing our development actions. Let us now consider how we might respond to the development actions we might have identified.

DEVELOPMENTAL OPPORTUNITIES

Once we have identified our development needs, we can explore the various ways to fulfil them. There is a tendency to forget the array of developmental opportunities available to us beyond the most commonly cited methods, which include attending a course, a seminar or a conference. These learning opportunities provide legitimate ways of filling a knowledge gap but they are by no means the only ways. How might knowledge be applied back in the workplace? If funds are more limited, other interventions may be required. Let us explore ideas for supporting our identified development goals.

Courses, seminars and conferences

Attending courses, seminars, short courses and conferences can be a great way of filling a skills or knowledge gap. Whether they last an hour or several days, formal programmes provide an intensive form of professional updating. These events can also provide opportunities for networking with like-minded professionals. Having said this, some professionals find it difficult to dedicate considerable time to formal programmes, and courses can also be expensive. They are scheduled to take place at specific times for a defined duration. The key question is: what will you gain from your investment? Perhaps you need a certificate, an accreditation or badge? If not, you might explore other ways to meet your development needs, as discussed below. Relevant programmes might be offered through your HR professional body, e.g. the SHRM or CIPD. You might also explore private training providers in your local area, such as local universities and colleges.

E-learning

The opportunities for self-paced e-learning are increasing at a rapid pace. If you have identified a knowledge or skills gap and you find it difficult to find the time to attend formal events with prescriptive attendance requirements, e-learning can be a very accessible alternative. LinkedIn Learning provides a wide range of video-based business programmes, and Coursera is constantly updating its offering, which currently stands at more than 3,000 programmes.[58] These courses can be studied in your own time, at a pace that suits you. Although course fees vary, e-learning programmes such as those mentioned above increasingly offer a subscription service so that you are able to access as many programmes as you desire. However, bear in mind that although e-learning platforms provide flexible professional development opportunities, they seldom offer effective ways to build networks.

Formal qualifications

You may have identified that you need to gain specific qualifications for your role or the role that you aspire to, particularly professional people-related certifications. Refer back to chapter 4 for full details on how to get qualified. Formal qualifications require an investment of both time and money but they can be essential for career progression.

Professional body activities

A range of developmental opportunities and events are offered by professional bodies, and many of these are free because they are included in your professional body membership fees. It is a good idea to attend events and even to share your own knowledge and skills. Teaching others is a great way to reinforce your own understanding of skills and knowledge. This can help you build your network as well as your professional expertise.

Web groups

A web group is an online community where members are able to exchange content, including articles, information and news about a topic of shared interest. Belonging to a web group can provide access to specialist knowledge and experts in specific areas. This can be helpful for sharing good practice and building networks.

Shadowing

Job shadowing is helpful for gaining real insights into the work of others by spending time with them and observing and engaging with them in their everyday work. Shadowing can be helpful for both parties because the questions posed can encourage fresh analysis of taken-for-granted activities. It is also great for networking. The specific arrangements for shadowing can be arranged between the parties involved. There are different forms of shadowing: some are limited to observation, while others provide opportunities for active involvement. Early in my career I spent a week at the University of Cambridge, learning how it delivers its Grad School. On the first day I observed, on the second and third days I *supported* delivery, and on the last two days I *led* delivery. Regular briefings supported the transfer of learning, with a final debrief to cement key points on my final day.

Action learning

Action learning is a process for bringing thinking and action together. It is a problem-solving technique that focuses on action and reflection. Through reflection we gain a deeper understanding of the issues we face, enabling us to manage change more effectively. Working in diverse groups with people from your own organization or with professionals from different organizations in an action learning set can be helpful not only for enhancing leadership and management skills but also for increasing confidence. Action learning sets can take place in person or virtually. The originator of action learning sets was Professor Reginald Revans, who found that setting up a small group of people to share their experiences and problems with the purpose of finding a solution was an effective method of learning and problem-solving.[59] You might like to explore existing action learning set opportunities in your current organization or to set one up if your employer does not already have one. You might also like to discuss action learning sets with your professional body.

Reading

There are many books that have a big influence on the way we lead our lives, guiding our professional practice and helping us explore opportunities. Reading is a very valid way to enhance our knowledge and skills. You might consult reviews or dedicated people management sites that offer their top ten reading choices, or you might follow up on key themes related to the knowledge and skills gaps that you have identified. You might also read professional journals and magazines. Ensure that sources are contemporary and that data are current.

Coaching and mentoring

It may be possible to secure a coach or mentor through your organization or professional body. Coaching is a process that can unlock your potential in order to maximize your performance. It is usually short term and used for specific objectives. Over the years I have coached many people in support of transitioning to a new career, securing a new role, developing leadership and more specific areas such as time management, returning to work and influencing people. Mentors can support, guide and advise you, and they tend to share their experience of different situations to support more generic professional and leadership development. Having a coach or mentor can be invaluable for securing career advancement.

WHICH METHOD SHOULD I CHOOSE?

Now that you are familiar with the various ways you might respond to your identified learning needs, consider the time you have available that you can dedicate to updating. How flexible are you? What is your preferred learning style? Which of the follows methods do you find more effective: watching a video, listening to a podcast, attending a formal course, reading a book, talking with others or learning on the job? You might like to reflect on the methods that have been most effective for you in the past, but bear in mind that our preferences can change over time. Many of my students were very reluctant to learn online prior to the Covid-19 pandemic and yet, when I offered them the opportunity to return to class, they had adapted to online learning and were reluctant to go back to normal!

Now let us consider an example of a development plan that details identified development needs, the steps towards achieving them (developmental intervention), the required resources or support, the way success will be measured, and finally the intended target date for completion.

Case study

Rebecca is keen to advance from an administration role in the people team to a business partner role. She has been searching for vacancies and exploring the role requirements, person specification and associated competencies for a people business partner. She is keen to work in the professional services area, perhaps with lawyers, accountants, management consultants or similar. Ideally, she is looking for an organization that supports hybrid working so that she can balance her work and life more effectively. Rebecca has undertaken a SWOT analysis of her current skill set and aligned this with her ideal next role by compiling a development audit. She would like to work in an organization that recognizes achievement and provides opportunities for further development.

Rebecca is looking for a culture that is professional, happy and innovative because this aligns with her definition of success, which is based on working for an organization that provides a healthy work–life balance while offering an innovative and fun environment in which to flourish. Rebecca is keen for a role that encourages autonomy, stretching goals, opportunities for promotion and ongoing development.

Rebecca has compiled a development plan (see figure 9) to summarize her identified key developmental actions.

Reflection

A key part of navigating our professional development is to reflect on our journey so far. What is your career story? Consider your professional experience, skills and academic background. What sets you apart from other professionals? What are your core values? You might like to include references to your hobbies and interests. It is a great way of reviewing your whole self and the distance you have travelled so far. It will help you identify and prioritize your learning and development goals.

Reflecting on our skills, knowledge and behaviours is an essential part of informing our CPD, enabling us to turn our self-assessments into workable goals, objectives and development plans. Having clear objectives in place, monitoring these and reflecting on our progress enables us to advance our career.

But what does reflection really mean? Reflection is about focusing on what has gone well, on what has not gone so well, and on any potential development and actions needed. Just because an event went well does not mean further reflection on development opportunities does not need to take place. Focus on what went well and why (for example, an interview might go well one day when

Name: Rebecca Malloy				
Start date: November 2021				**End date**: October 2022
Identified development need	**How will this be achieved?**	**What resources/ support will be required?**	**How will I measure success?**	**Target date for completion and review**
To learn about technological developments in the people profession	Attend the 2022 HR Disrupted summit that will focus on technological advancements in the people profession	Permission from my current company to attend and investment	Improved understanding of how to use technology to reduce the transactional activity in my current role	August 2022
To expand my strategic remit by gaining experience assessing, devising and implementing strategy in another sector	Become a CIPD enterprise advisor (volunteer) so that I work in partnership with a school to develop their careers strategy	8 hours a month to dedicate to the partnership and support from others in the enterprise network including the CIPD and other advisors	Successful contribution to the school's career strategy with positive feedback from school staff	October 2022
To achieve promotion to become people business partner	Build my network with senior stakeholders through current organization, LinkedIn and professional body; focus on value added by my contribution; develop strategic insights through voluntary work	Time and determination; feedback from stakeholders that will help me to build my development plan	Promotion to the role of people business partner	October 2022
To gain greater awareness of financial health of current organization in order to add value	Request one-to-one session with our head of finance to understand profit and loss and inter-departmental budgets	Support of the head of finance and an opportunity to put knowledge into practice	Increased confidence in discussing financial issues in an organizational context	March 2022

Figure 9 An example professional development plan.

you are lucky with the type of questions asked), and then determine which knowledge and behaviours you used to ensure the event went well. Share your experiences with colleagues, mentors or friends, who might provide a new perspective on the event. Do the same for activities that do not go so well. After reflection comes action. Action involves setting targets and timescales, finding the necessary resources and support, and planning review periods, as well as knowing when your objectives have been achieved. This is the basis of your development plan.

We can engage in reflective thinking when we step back and consider an experience. We need to think about what happened, what we did and why. It is important to assess the rationale for your actions: why you did what you did (or did not do). What might you do differently in the future? Engaging in reflective thinking helps us to take responsibility for our own learning and ensures that we are equipped to take full advantage of study and learning opportunities. It helps us in our professional practice by supporting us in making sense of new and unexplained situations.

The best way to engage in reflective thinking and writing is to engage in ideas generation. Take some notes about your experiences when the details, thoughts and emotions are still fresh in your mind.

Top tip

I often encourage my learners to keep a reflective diary of key learning that takes place across programmes, in organizations and during self-directed updating. Whether it is kept in hard copy or soft copy, it is a good idea to get into the habit of reflecting on your key achievements each week, including what went well, what went less well and what were the key areas of learning. This provides a very helpful base from which to inform further developmental work.

Analyse your experience by taking a step back, to gain a sense of perspective. Look at any significant trends and patterns. Ask yourself questions. What are the implications of what you have learnt?

Reflective questions

- What was the event/situation?
- What did you do?

- Who else was involved?
- What role did others take?
- How were you feeling (before, during and after the event/situation)?
- How were others feeling?
- What was good/bad about the event/situation?
- What went well/not so well?
- What else could you have done?
- What else could others have done?
- What would you do next time in a similar situation?
- What are the key actions to support your future development?

These questions are inspired by the models of Gibbs's reflective cycle[60] and Borton's model of reflection.[61]

The reflective work that you have engaged in so far can be captured in a professional development record. Compiling your reflections provides a summary document that can support professional membership upgrades and job applications. You will have all the details you require ready as and when you need them.

Now let us take a look at a completed professional development record that has been compiled using the reflective diary and notes discussed above: see figure 10 overleaf.

Having reviewed examples of a CPD plan and record in this chapter, perhaps you might like to now compile your own?

Activity: CPD plan

Hopefully, by working through the exercises in this chapter you now feel confident in producing your own CPD plan. You might like to use the format in the earlier example (figure 9) as a framework, or you can design one yourself. There is no single right way to present your CPD: it is about what works most effectively for you.

Name: Rebecca Malloy				
Start date: November 2020				**End date**: November 2021
Date of development	**Development activity**	**Why did I undertake this?**	**What did I learn from this?**	**How will I use this?**
Nov 2020–Nov 2021	I supported my line manager in the roll out of the new HR system. I liaised with IT, employees and contractors to ensure that the training was in place and delivered in a timely manner.	This was my first project in the people team. The opportunity allowed me to develop my project management skills.	I learnt that I was capable of managing a large project with multiple stakeholders. I developed skills in seeking budget approval.	This project has provided me with the platform to build relationships with stakeholders across the business, including the CEO, head of finance, employees and contractors. Understanding the remit of these stakeholders in more detail will help me manage future projects more effectively.
Dec 2020	I attended the CIPD update on employmnent law.	I am the first point of contact for many people-related enquiries in my organzation. I would like to be able to respond to some of the basic enquiries more effectively and to prepare myself for future senior roles.	The update covered the role of tribunals, contractual issues, data protection and discrimination. It also provided an introduction to compromise agreements.	I have been able to support the people team more effectively by directing calls to specific policies. I am able to support colleagues in relation to contract matters.
Mar 2021	I asked for a performance management review.	I wanted to gain feedback about my progress so far. I was particularly keen to learn about how I can develop. I also asked three stakeholers for feedback.	Feedback was positive. It gave me confidence to continue with the way I was undertaking my role.	The positive feedback is good but I will now work on stretching my capabilities further so that I can effectively prepare for promotion. I will use the professional body competency framework to help me.

Figure 10 An example continuing professional development record.

Activity: CPD record

Think back over the last year and consider what development activities you have engaged in. Remember to include everything:

courses, conferences, webinars, mentoring, coaching, secondments, shadowing, digital learning, reading, community groups, networks, projects and collaborations.

SUMMARY

CPD is not something that you aim to *complete*. Rather, it is a live document that you update regularly as you gain more experience and progress in your career. CPD is a journey of exploration rather than a destination, and it will evolve as your career develops. Although some professionals may argue that their CPD is driven by their employer, personally I disagree. CPD is something that each of us should take responsibility for. Your organization has their own agenda for your development: namely, ensuring that you are equipped effectively to deliver its strategic plan. CPD informs your personal career strategy so that you focus on looking forward and, potentially, on transferring your learning. CPD is also a great way to learn lessons from your experiences as it helps you to re-analyse your initial thoughts with the aim of gaining deeper insights. It is essential for upgrading your professional body membership and it is very helpful in supporting your job search.

Chapter 11

FURTHER RESOURCES AND SUPPORT

THERE IS AN ABUNDANCE OF resources and information that will help you to build your knowledge of the people management profession. Whether you are new to the profession or looking to advance to your next role, I hope that the selection of my favourite sources listed below will be helpful. A word of caution, though: the people profession is evolving very quickly and it is important to stay up to date in order to have the very best chance of securing your preferred role. You might like to put aside some time each week to check on the latest developments.

BOOKS

The list that follows contains useful books that provide an introduction to the subject. Some of these provide a fantastic overview of all elements of HR, while others focus on particular areas of people management.

Armstrong's Handbook of Human Resource Management **by Michael Armstrong with Stephen Taylor (Kogan Page, 2020)**
I recommend this great introduction to the subject of HR to all my undergraduate learners. If you are new to the discipline it provides an overview of the core themes throughout the employee lifecycle.

Armstrong is one of the UK's bestselling authors of HR management books, having sold more than a million copies.

***Resourcing and Talent Management* by Stephen Taylor (Kogan Page, 2018)**

This provides an in-depth exploration of how to effectively resource an organization and how to manage talent over the employee life-cycle. Taylor is a senior lecturer in HR management at the University of Exeter's Business School. He previously held lecturing posts at Manchester Business School and at the Manchester Metropolitan University Business School. Before his academic career he worked in a variety of management roles in the hotel industry and in the UK's National Health Service. Stephen was previously chief examiner at the CIPD.

***Work and Employment in a Changing Business Environment* by Stephen Taylor and Graham Perkins (Kogan Page, 2021)**

This book provides a contemporary look at the current workplace and includes an introduction to key themes impacting the people profession. The book covers it all: globalization, technology, the economy and labour markets, population and society, politics, productivity, ethics and values, sustainability and corporate responsibility, well-being, and equality, diversity and inclusion. Taylor (see previous book) and Perkins are senior lecturers in HR management within the management department at the University of Exeter.

***HR Analytics Essentials* by Michael Walsh (Vibrant Publishers, 2021)**

Walsh provides an introduction to analytics and the ways in which we can present qualitative and quantitative information in the form of a story. The book includes helpful visuals in the form of charts and graphs, as well as case studies, discussion questions and quizzes. Including staffing, training and compensation, this book explores data across HR, providing a helpful framework to both understand and apply data in human resources. Walsh is an industrial and organizational psychologist with more than 15 years of HR and people analytics experience. He currently leads global talent management and organizational effectiveness for Eaton Corporation's Vehicle Group, as well as teaching an HR analytics course for master's-level students at the University of Illinois and Wayne State University.

***Wellbeing at Work* by Cary Cooper and Ian Hesketh (Kogan Page, 2019)**

This provides an effective framework for designing, implementing and evaluating an effective strategy. It addresses how to promote well-being in the workplace through resilience, engagement and training. It explores challenges associated with workplace well-being and how to respond through the monitoring and evaluation of efficiency, productivity, performance and happiness. Professor Sir Cary Cooper, CBE, is a professor of organizational psychology and health at Alliance Manchester Business School, University of Manchester, and he is president of the CIPD. Hesketh is the Wellbeing Lead at the UK College of Policing and the Senior Responsible Owner for the National Police Wellbeing Service in the UK.

***People Practice: A Complete Guide* by Karen Waite, Kathy Beevers, Nicky Small, Keith Tomlinson and Shazad Hussain (Kogan Page, 2021)**

This is written in support of the CIPD level 3 qualification in people practice. It provides the core theory and practice to support an understanding of key areas in HR, including business, culture, change in context and workforce analytics. It also covers core skills, external factors that impact organizations, ethical and inclusive practice, and how all of these areas relate to recruitment, performance, reward and supporting others. The book is written by the team that developed the qualification so it ensures that learners are effectively prepared for the programme. It is also a great resource for school leavers and graduates who would like an introductory and easy-to-follow text.

***Learning and Development Practice in the Workplace* by Kathy Beevers, Andrew Rea and David Hayden (Kogan Page, 2020)**
This is a great read for all those with an interest in learning and development. It provides comprehensive insight into the role of the learning and development professional and its organizational context. The book explores each area of the learning and development cycle, including identifying learning and development needs, designing learning and development activities and delivering learning face to face, through methods such as technology, coaching and mentoring, social learning and collaborative learning. Very importantly, the book discusses how to evaluate learning in order to assess the impact it has had.

***Data-driven HR* by Bernard Marr (Kogan Page, 2018)**
This was a finalist in the HR and Management category of the 2019 Business Book Awards. It explains what data-driven HR is and then goes on to describe how data can be used to support the business case for it. The book explores data-driven strategies, data privacy, transparency and security. It then considers how data is used in recruitment, employee engagement, learning and development, employee wellness and performance management. Two really helpful features of this book are the case studies and the real-life examples, which help people professionals use data in a way that genuinely adds value and makes a difference in their respective

organizations. For those seeking to gain entry into the profession, it is this knowledge and understanding that will really help you to stand out from the crowd.

***The Squiggly Career* by Helen Tupper and Sarah Ellis (Penguin Random House, 2020)**

This is a *Sunday Times* bestseller in the business category. It is packed with careers advice, focusing on possibilities and exploring values, confidence and networks. It also addresses some of those personal quandaries that we often experience: when to change job, how to find a mentor and how to achieve work–life balance. It also includes signposting to a number of helpful sources that will help you reflect on your life and career and plan for tomorrow.

***Agile HR: Deliver Value in a Changing World of Work* by Natal Dank and Riina Hellström (Kogan Page, 2020)**

This is one of my personal favourites. Agile HR is conceived in this book as an incremental development cycle: plan, do, check and act. It is about experimentation and prototyping to continuously test what works and what does not. The book argues that best practice can be too static and it suggests a blueprint for one-size-fits-all HR processes and systems. Dank leads on learning, coaching and community at PXO Culture and is seen as a pioneer in the agile HR movement. Hellström is an agile people professional who has led innovation in the field of agile HR since 2010.

SOCIAL MEDIA

A huge amount of content is posted daily, so you will certainly be able to build your own favourites list to help you with your people profession development. This is also a great way to start collaborating in order to raise your profile in the profession.

Instagram

There are more than 200 million business accounts on Instagram and more than a billion users around the world sharing content every day via www.instagram.com. You will learn not only from businesses here but also from many independent consultants and professionals. This is a great way to learn more about specific areas in the profession through tailored case study examples. You might like to follow leading organizations in the field of HR such as @deloitte, which provides great insights into the evolving nature of the profession.

LinkedIn

LinkedIn is the world's largest professional network on the internet. As well as offering the opportunity to connect with a wide range of people professionals, the platform also includes details of upcoming events that are relevant to you based on your profile and any posts that you make. You can also keep up to date with your favourite influencers (I follow Daniel Goleman, for instance, and his work on emotional intelligence) and companies (here I follow *Harvard Business Review* and CIPD Middle East).

Hashtags

A hashtag is a word or phrase used on social media websites and applications to support the cross-referencing of content. Each time I post on LinkedIn, for example, I use a number of hashtags that relate to the subject of the post (e.g. employee experience). If you wish to search for, say, HR salaries, you could search using #HRSalaries. With so much content being posted every day you will certainly find plenty of results, although you might find it a challenge to find exactly what you are looking for due to the sheer volume of posts!

Twitter

Twitter provides an immediate and intimate connection with people professionals and can be a great way to keep in touch with professionals and academics you are following. I recently took part in a tweet chat with colleagues from the UK National Health Service on the subject of 'ethical recruitment'. A tweet chat is where you schedule a time to discuss a subject with others. We advertised the event across all social media so that everyone had the opportunity to connect and discuss. This can be a great way of raising your profile and ensuring that influential people know who you are.

Blogging

Blogging is another great way to raise your profile and your global reach in support of your job applications. Start by commenting on other blogs so that you build an online presence. Take a look at platforms such as Blogger, WordPress and Wix. The basic sites are free so you can start sharing posts immediately.

WEBSITES

People Management

This is is the journal of the CIPD (see www.peoplemanagement.co.uk). Packed full of news, commentary, updates and jobs, it is worth reviewing this site regularly. Non-members can review quite a bit of content for free, including interviews and the latest news, by accessing the website or signing up for weekday emails.

Personnel Today

This is a UK free-access HR website (www.personneltoday.com) that provides people professionals with up-to-date news, analysis and specialist advice, including topical content, awards, jobs and webinars. It is a very useful site from which to learn about practice-based HR. It contains some useful coverage of UK employment law issues, along with case study examples, to help you keep abreast of workplace developments.

HR Zone

This is an online human resources publication (www.hrzone.com). It is designed to help global HR professionals keep up to date with the evolving nature of the people profession in a rapidly changing world. The website is full of case study examples that provide insights into topical issues.

Professional body websites

More generally, the professional body websites discussed in this book are great platforms from which to keep up to date and to gain deeper insights into HR. However, as mentioned above it is a good idea to keep abreast of the evolving nature of the profession through a combination of sources to avoid a one-dimensional perspective.

TED TALKS

TED is a non-profit organization that is committed to sharing great ideas in the form of short, powerful talks (www.ted.com/talks). A wide spectrum of speakers present on a diverse range of topics. Here are some interesting talks relevant to the HR profession.

Dan Pink: 'The puzzle of motivation'

Dan Pink is a career analyst who explores the puzzle of motivation through a series of stories that suggest traditional rewards are not as effective as we think.

Rainer Strack: 'The workforce crisis of 2030 – and how to start solving it now'

By 2030 the world's largest economies will have more jobs than citizens. In this talk, which is amply supported by data, Strack, an HR expert, encourages us to think about organizational culture as we recruit from different talent pools.

Margaret Heffernan: 'Forget the pecking order at work'

Organizations do not have ideas, people do. That is why it is so important to understand what drives high-performing teams. Rather than placing value on star employees who outperform others, Heffernan suggests that we look at effective team dynamics and behaviour.

Mary Schaefer: 'Putting the human back into human resources'

This topic is a passion of mine: reminding ourselves that HR is about people. This talk looks at how we can create work cultures where both organizations and human beings can thrive and where everyone in an organization can be heard.

Carol Dweck: 'The power of believing that you can improve'

Dweck is a psychologist best known for her work on the growth mindset: the idea that we can grow our brain's capacity to learn and to solve problems. If we apply this idea to people in organizations, we can fundamentally change the way in which we design and deliver learning and development.

A list of other TED talks that I direct students and aspiring people professionals to follows below:

- https://www.ted.com/talks/marco_alvera_the_surprising_ingredient_that_makes_businesses_work_better
- https://www.ted.com/talks/nigel_marsh_how_to_make_work_life_balance_work
- https://www.ted.com/talks/amy_cuddy_your_body_language_may_shape_who_you_are?language=en
- https://www.ted.com/talks/cara_e_yar_khan_the_beautiful_balance_between_courage_and_fear#t-583410
- https://www.ted.com/talks/amy_edmondson_how_to_turn_a_group_of_strangers_into_a_team
- https://www.ted.com/talks/michael_c_bush_this_is_what_makes_employees_happy_at_work?language=en&referrer=playlist-the_way_we_work
- https://www.ted.com/talks/celeste_headlee_10_ways_to_have_a_better_conversation
- https://www.ted.com/talks/tim_urban_inside_the_mind_of_a_master_procrastinator
- https://www.ted.com/talks/alan_iny_reigniting_creativity_in_business
- https://www.ted.com/talks/patrice_gordon_how_reverse_mentorship_can_help_create_better_leaders
- https://www.ted.com/talks/diana_laufenberg_how_to_learn_from_mistakes

PODCASTS

There is now such an extensive choice of audio that you will certainly have no difficulty in finding content on a subject that interests you. The great thing about podcasts is that you can listen to them while doing something else – even while travelling or resting. University academics are increasingly developing content to support open lecture series and to share their research. For example, my friend and colleague Dr Steve McKenna (Associate Professor of Management at Curtin Business School, Curtin University in Perth Australia) has developed the 'Disrupting HR' series, which is available on Anchor by Spotify (https://anchor.fm/steve-mckenna4/). In the series Steve challenges taken-for-granted assumptions about HR.

You might also like to explore the following podcasts that my colleagues and I often include in our reading lists for students. The podcasts are directed at students studying CIPD programmes and are therefore designed in alignment with these programmes. It is a good idea to utilize sources from a wide range of media to ensure a balanced and international perspective. This will help you to prepare more effectively for the future of work and learning.

- https://www.cipd.co.uk/podcasts/evidence-based-hr
- https://www.cipd.co.uk/podcasts/critical-thinking
- https://www.cipd.co.uk/podcasts/od-questionable-truths
- https://www.cipd.co.uk/podcasts/resilience
- https://www.cipd.co.uk/podcasts/ethical-workplaces
- https://www.cipd.co.uk/podcasts/hr-business-ethics
- https://www.cipd.co.uk/podcasts/ethics-leadership
- https://www.cipd.co.uk/podcasts/trust
- https://www.cipd.co.uk/podcasts/building-best-team
- https://www.cipd.co.uk/podcasts/shifting-perception-conflict
- https://www.cipd.co.uk/podcasts/social-learning
- https://www.cipd.co.uk/podcasts/self-directed-learning
- https://www.cipd.co.uk/podcasts/cpd-for-hr
- https://www.cipd.co.uk/podcasts/neuroscience-on-insight-intuition-creativity
- https://www.cipd.co.uk/podcasts/new-learning-organisation

YOUTUBE

YouTube (www.youtube.com) is an American online video-sharing and social media platform. It includes a huge amount of content related to every aspect of HR. Many lectures are now filmed and uploaded to the platform, as are personal insights into the profession from those working in senior HR roles. In training and academic programmes I use short clips from YouTube to offer different perspectives. Look out for key themes such as future projections about the world of work in order to keep yourself abreast of developments.

NEWSPAPERS AND MAGAZINES

One of my favourite weekly publications is *The Economist* (www.economist.com). It contains a wealth of information, from a global perspective, ensuring that I keep abreast of developments in political, economic, social, technological, cultural and environmental matters. It is a great resource for aspiring HR professionals and for those who are seeking to progress to senior positions.

Harvard Business Review (www.hbr.org) is very good for general management, and it balances new ideas with fundamental principles in strategy, innovation and leadership. It is aimed at business leaders and provides an organizational perspective rather than an HR focus – this is very useful for partnering with businesses and advancing your career in organizations.

For those interested in a career in recruitment, *Recruiter* (www.recruiter.co.uk) covers everything from in-house resourcing to agency recruitment. Online content is free.

The HR Director (www.thehrdirector.com) is aimed at HR directors and senior practitioners, and it includes exclusive interviews with senior HR professionals in large organizations. This is a useful resource when preparating for more senior roles.

Training Journal (www.trainingjournal.com) is a great resource for learning and development professionals and for those hoping to enter the profession. From apprenticeships to coaching, facilitation and organizational development, this journal covers a wide range of topics and can be useful for HR professionals too.

JOURNALS

Aside from the professional magazines and websites discussed above, you might like to review academic journals. It is increasingly possible to view papers through open-access content, which means that they are free to read. Some very good journals in HR management include the following:

- *Human Resource Management*
- *Journal of Business Ethics*
- *Journal of Management*
- *Journal of Management Studies*
- *Journal of Managerial Psychology*
- *Journal of Vocational Behavior*
- *Organization Studies*
- *Organization and Work*
- *Employment and Society*

Google Scholar (https://scholar.google.com) is an effective search tool for finding free articles. It is also worth searching for the author of the article you are interested in as the paper may be freely available to download from www.researchgate.net. If you are studying at university, you will be able to source journal articles through your institution's library.

SUMMARY

The best way to find out about a career in HR is to get some direct experience in a role, but the resources in this chapter will prepare you thoroughly for work experience and job applications. Do engage in networking, as discussed in this book, through a professional body or a local business group. Also, connect with people professionals via LinkedIn by asking questions and building your profile. Read widely across a range of sources to gain an international perspective.

ENDNOTES

1 CIPD. 2021. Our history. Web page (www.cipd.co.uk/about/who-we-are/history).

2 S. Tyson and A. Fell. 1986. *Evaluating the Personnel Function*. London: Hutchinson.

3 TUC. 2021. The role of the union representative. Report (www.tuc.org.uk/resource/role-union-representative).

4 ONS. 2015. The history of strikes in the UK. Web article, 21 September (https://bit.ly/3heGKNS).

5 F. W. Taylor. 1911. *The Principles of Scientific Management*. London: Harper and Brothers.

6 A. H. Maslow. 1943. A theory of human motivation. *Psychological Review* **50**, 370–396. A. H. Maslow. 1954. *Motivation and Personality*. London: Harper and Brothers.

7 Reed. 2021. Reed salary guides 2021. Online tool (www.reed.com/tools/reed-salary-guides-2021).

8 Bureau of Labor Statistics/US Department of Labor. 2020. Human resources managers. In *Occupational Outlook Handbook*. BLS (www.bls.gov/ooh/management/human-resources-managers.htm).

9 SHRM. 2021. HR professional body website: www.shrm.org/.

10 CIPD. 2021. HR professional body website: www.cipd.co.uk/.

11 SHRI. 2021. HR professional body website: https://shri.org.sg/about-us/shri/.

12 IHRMP. 2018. HR professional body website: www.ihrmp.com/.

13 AHRI. 2021. HR professional body website: www.ahri.com.au/.

14 R. Bolton. 2020. Lessons for HR. Blog post, KPMG (https://bit.ly/3ELpREp).

15 Visier. 2015. Visier customer forum to feature acclaimed HR thought leader. Press Release, 28 August (https://bit.ly/3CHxji9).

16 M. Nevins. 2019. What is the purpose of a company? *Forbes Magazine*, 28 August (https://bit.ly/3ugbeEs).

17 Bright Network. 2021. Human resources internship 2021. Jobs website (https://bit.ly/2ZmG0Qp).

18 ZipRecruiter. 2021. Amazon human resources internship. Jobs website (https://bit.ly/3EPpgBO).
19 WIZBII. 2021. Human resource intern. An internship with General Electric. Jobs website (https://bit.ly/3ADg3K5).
20 CharityJob. 2021. HR assistant voluntary role. Jobs website (www.charityjob.co.uk/hr-administrator-jobs).
21 EthicalJobs. 2021. Volunteer coordinator. Jobs website (https://bit.ly/3nZvjxD).
22 Job\Searcher. 2021. Recruitment coordinator. Jobs website (https://bit.ly/3lNL9IM).
23 Glassdoor. 2021. 50 HR & recruitment stats that make you think! Blog post, 20 January (https://bit.ly/3i2LmqI).
24 S. Purewal. 2018. Does your CV pass the seven second test? Blog post, Reed (https://bit.ly/3EOt6ej).
25 LinkedIn. 2020. How do I create a good LinkedIn profile? Web page, 31 March (https://bit.ly/3CC9msq).
26 SHRM. 2021. Jobs. HR professional body website: www.jobs.shrm.org.
27 CIPD. 2021. PM jobs. HR professional body website: www.pmjobs.cipd.co.uk.
28 A. Stirling. 2021. Stirling Careers Consultancy website: www.stirlingcareersconsultancy.co.uk.
29 Jobvite. 2021. Jobs website: www.jobvite.com/.
30 SHL. 2021. Practice tests. Web page (www.shl.com/shldirect/en/practice-tests).
31 IBM. 2021. AI can help transform HR in three key ways. Report (https://ibm.co/3i2KUss).
32 XOR. 2018. Case study on how IKEA decreased candidate drop-off rate. Web page (www.xor.ai/ikea-case-study).
33 S. Harris and E. Spencer. 2019. Sierra-Cedar 2018–2019 HR Systems Survey White Paper, 21st Annual Edition. White Paper (https://bit.ly/3AS4sr3).
34 G. Lahiri, E. Volini and J. Schwaraz. 2018. People data: how far is too far? *Deloitte Insights*, 28 March (https://bit.ly/3EOtSbd).
35 ICO. 2021. Personal data breaches. Web page (https://bit.ly/3tqRY6N).
36 Department for Work and Pensions. 2017. Fuller working lives: evidence base 2017. Report, February (https://bit.ly/38Qd0lP).
37 Office for National Statistics. 2020. Female employment rate (aged 16 to 64, seasonally adjusted). Report, 16 June (https://bit.ly/2Y2K9J8).
38 B. Hamer. 2020. Why attracting and retaining the top millennial talent is key to future success. Blog post, 23 July, PWC (https://pwc.to/3o2V0gB).

39 SOM. 2021. B&Q and ageing workers. Blog post (www.som.org.uk/bq-and-ageing-workers).
40 Office for National Statistics. 2020. Employment, unemployment and economic inactivity by age group. Data set (https://bit.ly/2X9x93K).
41 Oxford Economics. 2021. Global Talent 2021. Report (https://bit.ly/3CJ4bHm).
42 International Labour Organization. 2020. World employment and social outlook: trends 2020. Report (https://bit.ly/3AKwQeE).
43 PWC. 2020. Navigating the rising tide of uncertainty. 23rd Annual Global CEO Survey (https://pwc.to/2XKA2YK).
44 Corporate Rebels. 2021. Ditch annual performance reviews: here's how Netflix did it. Blog post (https://bit.ly/3i2N6QM).
45 McKinsey & Company. 2018. Delivering through diversity. Report, January (https://mck.co/3hB5wYL).
46 Apple. 2021. We're all in. Inclusion and Diversity web page (www.apple.com/diversity/).
47 McKinsey & Company. 2018. The five trademarks of agile organizations. Report, 22 January (https://mck.co/2W6PyxK).
48 J. Sutherland. 2017. The Boston Consulting Group: pushing the art and science of workplace design. Blog post, *Insight Magazine* (https://bit.ly/2XHAt6f).
49 C. Castrillon. 2020. This is the future of remote work in 2021. *Forbes Magazine*, 27 December (https://bit.ly/3oiaOfV).
50 A. McCulloch. 2021. Google plans return to office from September. Blog post, 1 April, *Personnel Today* (https://bit.ly/3ADPZyP).
51 J. Kelly. 2020. Siemens says that 140,000 of its employees can work from home anywhere. *Forbes Magazine*, 27 July (https://bit.ly/2W7TdeK).
52 CIPD. 2020. Homeworking set to more than double compared to pre-pandemic levels once crisis is over. Press Release, 16 July (www.cipd.co.uk/about/media/press/home-working-increases).
53 Deloitte. 2016. Transitioning to the future of work and the workplace. Analysis web page (https://bit.ly/2XPMOpA).
54 CIPD. 2020. People profession 2030. Report, November (https://bit.ly/3CWF3x1).
55 CIPD. 2021. About CIPD. Web page (www.cipd.co.uk/learn/cpd/about#gref).
56 CIPD. 2021. The profession map. Web page (https://peopleprofession.cipd.org/profession-map).
57 C. E. Ackerman. 2020. What is self-transcendence? Blog post, 18 February, *Positive Psychology* (https://positivepsychology.com/self-transcendence/).

58 Coursera is a global online learning platform that provides HR courses (www.coursera.org/courses?query=hr).
59 Action Learning Associates. 2021. Reg Revans. Web page (https://bit.ly/3EMUoBR).
60 University of Edinburgh. 2021. Gibbs' reflective cycle. Web page (https://bit.ly/3ADkEfj).
61 University of Nottingham. 2021. Driscoll (by Borton). Web page (on Borton's reflective model) (https://bit.ly/2XNjSyx).

ABOUT THE AUTHOR

Dr Kay Maddox-Daines is the founder of Future People Learning Ltd, head of the School for People and Culture at Arden University, and a Visiting Fellow at the University of Suffolk. Kay is also an external examiner for human resource management programmes at the American University in Greece and at Leeds Beckett University in the UK. She is a registered career development professional (RCDP) with the UK Career Development Institute, a member of the Chartered Institute of Personnel and Development (CIPD), a Fellow of the Chartered Management Institute (FCMI) and an executive career coach.

Previously, Kay worked as Director of Academic Development at Acacia Learning Ltd, overseeing accredited programmes in people management, and also as a leadership and career coach, a consultant and a senior manager in people management across the public and private sectors. Kay has taught, trained and coached professionals and executives in the UK, Eastern Europe, Gibraltar and the Middle East.

In her spare time Kay leads on people management matters as a non-executive director for the Sigma Trust, the largest multi-academy trust in Essex, which educates more than 11,000 pupils, employs 1,600 staff and has an annual income of more than £50 million. She also undertakes pro bono career coaching for aspiring people professionals and for those in career transition